WORLD
HISTORY SERIES ■ ■ ■

The Age of
Augustus

Titles in the World History Series

The Age of Augustus

by
Don Nardo

Lucent Books, P.O. Box 289011, San Diego, CA 92198-9011

Library of Congress Cataloging-in-Publication Data

Nardo, Don, 1947–
    The age of Augustus / by Don Nardo.
        p. cm. — (World history series)
    Includes bibliographical references and index.
Summary: Describes the politics, culture, religion, and society
of Rome during the reign of the Emperor Augustus.
    ISBN 1-56006-306-8 (alk. paper)
    1. Augustus, Emperor of Rome, 63 B.C.–14 A.D.—Influ-
ence—Juvenile literature. 2. Roman Emperors—Biography—
Juvenile literature. 3. Rome—History—Augustus, 30 B.C.–
14 A.D.—Juvenile literature. [1. Rome—History—Augustus,
30 B.C.–14 A.D.] I.Title. II. Series.
DG279.N37   1997
937'.07'092—dc20   96-14183
[B]   CIP
                                                    AC

Copyright 1997 by Lucent Books, Inc., P.O. Box 289011,
San Diego, California 92198-9011

Printed in the U.S.A.

Contents

Foreword

Each year on the first day of school, nearly every history teacher faces the task of explaining why his or her students should study history. One logical answer to this question is that exploring what happened in our past explains how the things we often take for granted—our customs, ideas, and institutions—came to be. As statesman and historian Winston Churchill put it, "Every nation or group of nations has its own tale to tell. Knowledge of the trials and struggles is necessary to all who would comprehend the problems, perils, challenges, and opportunities which confront us today." Thus, a study of history puts modern ideas and institutions in perspective. For example, though the founders of the United States were talented and creative thinkers, they clearly did not invent the concept of democracy. Instead, they adapted some democratic ideas that had originated in ancient Greece and with which the Romans, the British, and others had experimented. An exploration of these cultures, then, reveals their very real connection to us through institutions that continue to shape our daily lives.

Another reason often given for studying history is the idea that lessons exist in the past from which contemporary societies can benefit and learn. This idea, although controversial, has always been an intriguing one for historians. Those that agree that society can benefit from the past often quote philosopher George Santayana's famous statement, "Those who cannot remember the past are condemned to repeat it." Historians who ascribe to Santayana's philosophy believe that, for example, studying the events that led up to the major world wars or other significant historical events would allow society to chart a different and more favorable course in the future.

Just as difficult as convincing students to realize the importance of studying history is the search for useful and interesting supplementary materials that present historical events in a context that can be easily understood. The volumes in Lucent Books' World History Series attempt to present a broad, balanced, and penetrating view of the march of history. Ancient Egypt's important wars and rulers, for example, are presented against the rich and colorful backdrop of Egyptian religious, social, and cultural developments. The series engages the reader by enhancing historical events with these cultural contexts. For example, in *Ancient Greece*, the text covers the role of women in that society. Slavery is discussed in *The Roman Empire*, as well as how slaves earned their freedom. The numerous and varied aspects of everyday life in these and other societies are explored in each volume of the series. Additionally, the series covers the major political, cultural, and philosophical ideas as the torch of civilization is passed from ancient Mesopotamia and Egypt, through Greece, Rome, Medieval Europe, and other world cultures, to the modern day.

The material in the series is formatted in a thorough, precise, and organized manner. Each volume offers the reader a comprehensive and clearly written overview of an important historical event or period. The topic under discussion is placed in a broad historical context. For example, *The Italian Renaissance* begins with a discussion of the High Middle Ages and the loss of central control that allowed certain Italian cities to develop artistically. The book ends by looking forward to the Reformation and interpreting the societal changes that grew out of the Renaissance. Thus, students are not only involved in an historical era, but also enveloped by the events leading up to that era and the events following it.

One important and unique feature in the World History Series is the primary and secondary source quotations that richly supplement each volume. These quotes are useful in a number of ways. First, they allow students access to sources they would not normally be exposed to because of the difficulty and obscurity of the original source. The quotations range from interesting anecdotes to farsighted cultural perspectives and are drawn from historical witnesses both past and present. Second, the quotes demonstrate how and where historians themselves derive their information on the past as they strive to reach a consensus on historical events. Lastly, all of the quotes are footnoted, familiarizing students with the citation process and allowing them to verify quotes and/or look up the original source if the quote piques their interest.

Finally, the books in the World History Series provide a detailed launching point for further research. Each book contains a bibliography specifically geared toward student research. A second, annotated bibliography introduces students to all the sources the author consulted when compiling the book. A chronology of important dates gives students an overview, at a glance, of the topic covered. Where applicable, a glossary of terms is included.

In short, the series is designed not only to acquaint readers with the basics of history, but also to make them aware that their lives are a part of an ongoing human saga. Perhaps they will then come to the same realization as famed historian Arnold Toynbee. In his monumental work, *A Study of History,* he wrote about becoming aware of history flowing through him in a mighty current, and of his own life "welling like a wave in the flow of this vast tide."

Important Dates in the History of the Age of Augustus

B.C.	753	509	265	70	63	60	44	43	42	31	29	28	27

B.C.

753
Traditionally accepted date for the founding of Rome by the legendary Latin leader Romulus

509
Romans expel their king and establish the Roman Republic

265
After a long series of wars, the Romans control all of Italy south of the Po Valley

70
Augustan poet Virgil is born

63
Gaius Octavius the Younger, known as Octavian, who will one day bear the lofty title of Augustus Caesar, is born

60
Octavian's great-uncle Julius Caesar and two other powerful Romans, Pompey and Crassus, form an unofficial partnership—the First Triumvirate—and begin to impose their will on the government and the empire

44
After defeating Pompey in a bloody civil war and then declaring himself dictator for life, Caesar is assassinated by a group of disgruntled senators

43
In the wake of Caesar's demise, Octavian, only nineteen, unites with military generals Mark Antony and Marcus Lepidus to form the Second Triumvirate; to consolidate their power, the triumvirs murder hundreds of their political opponents; Augustan poet Ovid is born

42
Octavian and Antony defeat a republican army led by Caesar's assassins at Philippi, in northern Greece

31
After the collapse of the new triumvirate, Octavian, aided by his friend Marcus Agrippa, defeats Antony and his ally Cleopatra, queen of Egypt, in the sea battle of Actium, in western Greece

29
Octavian annexes Egypt as a Roman province; he celebrates three large triumphs, or victory parades, in Rome; Virgil completes the *Georgics*, a collection of poems about pastoral life; Octavian finishes and dedicates a new Senate House to replace the older one destroyed in a fire

28
Octavian renovates more than eighty religious temples

27

The Senate confers on Octavian the title of Augustus, "the revered and exalted one"; to celebrate the occasion, the senators change the month of *Sextilis* to Augustus (now August); Augustus launches his reign, dominated by his new autocratic political order, the *Principate*

23

Augustus is granted the considerable powers of the office of tribune, further strengthening his grip on the government; his beloved nephew Marcellus dies

20

Augustus makes peace with the Parthian Empire, removing a dangerous threat to the Roman Empire's eastern borders

19

Agrippa completes the Aqua Virga aqueduct; Virgil dies

18

Augustus pushes through a law making adultery a crime

17

The poet Horace composes the *Carmen saeculare* to commemorate the Secular Games, an ancient religious festival revived by Augustus

12

Lepidus, who was *pontifex maximus*, head of the Roman religion, dies and Augustus becomes pontiff; Agrippa dies; Augustus's stepson Drusus leads an army across the Rhine River into Germany

11

Augustus finishes and dedicates the Theater of Marcellus to honor his deceased nephew

A.D.
6

Augustus establishes a fire brigade, the *vigiles*, or "watchmen," for Rome; he heads off a famine by handing out free grain to the people

8

Augustus exiles the poet Ovid to a town on the Black Sea

9

A Roman army under Publius Varus is destroyed to the last man in a battle in a German forest

14

Augustus dies at the age of seventy-six; his stepson Tiberius becomes emperor

15

The Roman general Germanicus reaches the site of Varus's defeat and buries the bones of the dead

17

Ovid dies, signaling the end of the Augustan literary period

A Complex and Remarkable Individual

The term "Augustan Age" has been used at various times in history to describe a period of outstanding artistic and literary achievement in the life of a nation or people. One of the best-known such eras spanned the years from 1660 to 1744 in England. Producing many great literary works, including Jonathan Swift's *Gulliver's Travels* and the poems of Alexander Pope, the period is often referred to as the Augustan Age of English literature.

This and other similar rich literary ages are frequently compared to the original Augustan Age, the period of ancient Rome usually dated from 31 B.C. to A.D. 14. These forty-five years marked the eventful and highly fruitful reign of Augustus Caesar, the first in a long line of Roman emperors. Indeed, during his rule some of the greatest of all the Latin writers—the poets Virgil, Horace, and Ovid, and the historian Livy—produced numerous works still deemed masterpieces. Perhaps chief among these great artists was Virgil, who, in works such as the epic poem *Aeneid*, captured the essence of Rome's unique spirit, its conviction that it had a divine destiny to rule the world. "Virgil has many claims to greatness," writes scholar J. Wight Duff in *A Literary History of Rome:*

His amazing verbal art is one. His power to touch the feelings is another. His influence on [later] literature, and even his fame in the Middle Ages, are

This famous statue of Augustus Caesar, found at Prima Porta, near Rome, was carved during his fruitful forty-five-year reign by an unknown sculptor.

others still. . . . His poetic insight recognized the continuity of [Roman] Italy past and present . . . and recognized her queenship among the nations. To Virgil more than any other, the imperial grandeur of Rome was revealed.[1]

Yet great literature that would stand the test of time was not the only factor that made the Augustan Age extraordinary. It was also a time of bold political reform in which Rome, which had long been a republic dominated by an elite legislative body, the Senate, adopted a new, more dictatorial form of government dominated by a single man—Augustus himself. The traditional Roman Republic gave way to the experimental Roman Empire. It was the empire that would go on to transform the Mediterranean world and to lay the foundations for medieval and modern Europe.

It was also during the Augustan Age that Rome, long a dingy, graceless, and unattractive city, became the grand metropolis of polished marble that awed the world in the centuries that followed. Says historian Chester G. Starr:

> Augustus built a new Forum [public square], which had its center in a temple of Mars the Avenger [god of war]; around the edge of his Forum were statues of great heroes of Rome, including his own ancestors. In addition, he erected so many theaters, porticoes [column-lined porches and walkways], and other buildings that Rome began to be a truly great city.[2]

It was so great, in fact, that the ancient Greek geographer Strabo, who visited the city in its heyday, called it "a spectacle from which it is hard to tear yourself away." Strabo added, "Rome, which has exercised such magnetism over the centuries beyond all other cities, did so first in the days of Augustus."[3]

Augustus himself, a master of political propaganda, did not pass up the chance to sing his own praises. He boasted of his massive and splendid building programs in the *Res gestae*, the brief summary he left of his own achievements:

> I repaired the Capitol [the Capitoline Hill, on which rested temples of Jupiter, leader of the gods] and the theater of Pompey with enormous expenditures [of money] on both works, without having my name inscribed on them. I repaired the conduits of the aqueducts [stone structures that piped water] which were falling into ruin in many places. . . . I completed the Julian Forum and the basilica [stone meeting place] which was between the temple of Castor and the temple of Saturn [father of Jupiter and protector of farmers], works begun . . . by my father [his adoptive father, Julius Caesar].[4]

Augustus also bragged about the great sums he spent to stage public entertainments such as gladiator fights and replenish the state treasury during hard times, all from his own pocket.

In recognizing these and Augustus's many other substantial accomplishments, the driving force behind the greatness of the age named for him becomes clear. Many memorable historical periods are conveniently named for whatever ruler happens to be in power at the time, but not so with the Augustan Age. What made that age so exceptional was that Augustus

Augustus (seated at left with scroll) reads to a group of citizens in the Forum Romanum, Rome's busiest main square.

himself produced, motivated, or inspired nearly all of its great achievements. In *Rome in the Augustan Age*, classical historian Henry Thompson Rowell writes:

> About the Augustan Age it can be stated categorically that the complex of cultural and intellectual phenomena which we call Augustan culture would never have come into being and assumed the forms which it actually assumed without the towering figure of the Emperor. The spirit of national revival, the veneration of [reverence for] the glories of the past, the return to the ways and virtues of ancestors—all vigorously fostered by Augustus—struck a responsive chord in men of genius. In few periods have the sovereign [ruler] and most consummate [supremely skilled] artists worked together more harmoniously toward a high moral and patriotic goal.[5]

The only other comparable cultural golden age dominated by a single individual was the Periclean Age, in which fifth-century-B.C. Athens produced magnificent Greek art, architecture, and literature, works that awed and inspired later generations. And yet, even this analogy is inexact. The great Athenian statesman Pericles helped to create an atmosphere in which great artists and writers enjoyed financial and creative freedom. But he was not the absolute ruler of his age, as Augustus was of his own. Neither did Pericles set the moral and artistic standards for his society; nor did he project a godlike personal image that inspired artists to shower him with praises, as Augustus did.

Thus, to understand and appreciate the notable accomplishments of the Augustan Age, it is essential to understand the man who drove the age. He was without doubt one of the shrewdest, most ambitious, and most calculating politicians who ever lived. At the same time he was a simple man with a taste for fine culture and an intense, reverent respect for traditional Roman beliefs and values. This complex and remarkable individual—his life, goals, and rise to power in what was then the greatest empire in world history—must be the starting point for this examination of his unique age.

1 The Jungle of Roman Politics: Octavian's Rise to Ultimate Power

In a very real sense, Augustus Caesar's quest for ultimate power began even before his birth. His father, Gaius Octavius, belonged to the "equestrian order," an important social class made up mainly of well-to-do men who controlled Rome's commerce, industry, and financial institutions. But being an equestrian was not important enough for the ambitious Octavius. He dreamed of becoming a consul, the position of chief administrator/general that constituted the Roman state's highest government office. Traditionally, consuls were most often members of the patrician class. The patricians, whose wealth rested on landownership, and who represented the most ancient, distinguished, and powerful families, made up Rome's social and political nobility. Octavius realized that his best chance of gaining a consulship would be to marry into a patrician family.

And that is precisely what he did. In 65 B.C., Octavius married Atia, the daughter of Marcus Atias and his wife, Julia. It so happened that Julia's brother was the influential patrician politician Gaius Julius Caesar, who was already making a name for himself in government affairs and who, most people agreed, was himself destined to be consul. As Henry Rowell comments, in marrying Atia, Octavius had

made a crucial alliance, for the eminent Julii family line

> enjoyed all the power and prestige which the Octavii [Octavius's family] lacked. Its members traced their lineage back to the goddess Venus [deity of love and beauty] through her son

Julius Caesar (pictured), Octavian's great-uncle, had already become an important political figure by the time Octavian, the future Augustus, was born.

Aeneas, the founder of the Roman people, and his son Julius, from whom the family name was derived. Less mythical ancestors had held high positions in the state, including the consulship. In the year of the marriage, Atia's uncle, Gaius Julius Caesar, was . . . already an influential figure in Roman politics. It must have been obvious to the elder Octavius that he would make a very useful in-law.[6]

As it turned out, Julius Caesar became much more useful to Octavius's son. Gaius Octavius the Younger, who thereafter, thanks to his mother's kinship with the Julii, also bore the name of Caesar, was born on September 23, 63 B.C. The boy, who became known simply as Octavian, was short, very slight of build, and sickly. According to the Roman historian Suetonius, "He had a weakness in his left hip, thigh, and leg, which occasionally gave him the suspicion of a limp." Suetonius also reported that he "survived several grave and dangerous illnesses at different periods."[7] Certainly, no one at the time, including Octavian's great-uncle Caesar, could have suspected that this unassuming youth would one day be hailed as Augustus, "the most revered and exalted one," and reign unopposed over the known world.

Destiny of the Master Race

The world into which Octavian was born and which he came to know as he grew up was already stamped by the mark of Rome, which held sway over all the lands ringing the Mediterranean Sea. The city, already

One of the several surviving busts of the young Octavian. The second-century A.D. historian Suetonius claimed he owned a similar likeness, made of bronze, and that he gave it to the emperor Hadrian, who kept it in his own bedroom.

called "eternal" by its inhabitants, was located in west-central Italy on a bend in the Tiber River near the edge of the fertile plain of Latium. From the seven low hills on which the city rested, the Tiber wound its way about fifteen miles to the sea and Rome's port town of Ostia. There, cargo ships from all across Rome's empire regularly docked. They came from Spain in the far west, a land that bordered the vast uncharted reaches of the Atlantic Ocean; from Tunisia in northern Africa, once the site of the powerful trading city of Carthage before the Romans wiped it out of existence at the end of three brutal wars; from Asia Minor, what is now Turkey, which bordered the warm waters of the

Black Sea in the far east; as well as from Greece, grain-rich Egypt, and many other lands subservient to Rome's will.

The story of Rome's rise from humble beginnings to this position of great power and influence was epic, partly documented but to a large extent shrouded in mystery and legend. Like other young Romans, aristocrats and commoners alike, Octavian early learned the "whens," "hows," and "whos" of this eventful story and accepted most or all of it as fact. The first important "who" in the saga was Aeneas, a prince of the trading city of Troy, located in northwestern Asia Minor. When the Greeks sacked the city at the end of the fabled Trojan War, Aeneas supposedly escaped and sailed westward through the Mediterranean. Eventually he reached the western coast of Italy and established a set-

Serpents, Frogs, and Rainbows

Long after Octavian became the powerful ruler named Augustus, claims that omens occurred before, at, or after his birth became common. These supernatural signs, in which most ancient peoples, including the Romans, put great store, supposedly foretold Octavian's future greatness. The second-century-A.D. Roman historian Suetonius listed some of these signs, most of them clearly fanciful, in his biography of Augustus in Lives of the Twelve Caesars.

"Augustus's mother, Atia, with certain married women friends, once attended a solemn midnight service at the Temple of Apollo . . . and presently fell asleep as the others also did. Suddenly a serpent glided up, entered her, and then glided away again. On awakening, she purified [cleaned] herself, as if after intimacy with her husband. An irremovable colored mark in the shape of a serpent, which then appeared on her body, made her ashamed to visit the public baths any more; and the birth of Augustus nine months later suggested a divine paternity. . . . Once, when he was just learning to talk at his grandfather's [country house], the frogs broke into a loud chorus of croaking: he told them to stop, and it is locally claimed that no frog has croaked there since. On a later occasion, as he sat lunching . . . beside the Appian Way [the main road into Rome] . . . an eagle [symbol of Roman power], to his great surprise, swooped at him, snatched a crust from his hand, carried it aloft—and then, to his even greater surprise, glided gently down again and restored what it had stolen. . . . When he returned to Rome . . . at news of Caesar's assassination, the sky was clear of clouds, but a rainbow-like halo formed around the sun; and suddenly lightning struck the tomb of Caesar's daughter Julia."

tlement, Lavinium, Rome's parent city, situated about fifteen miles south of the Tiber. Later, in the first decade of the Augustan Age, Virgil would immortalize Aeneas and his achievement in his epic poem the *Aeneid*, beginning with the stirring words "Of arms I sing and the hero, destiny's exile, who came from the beach of Troy and was the first to make the Lavinian landfall, Italy."[8]

The following centuries in the legendary saga revolved around Aeneas's descendants, most importantly Romulus, who allegedly founded Rome itself in 753 B.C., the date now used to correspond with the year 1 of the Roman calendar.[9] Even at this early date, the Romans believed, their destiny to rule the world was already ordained by the gods. In Virgil's account, Jupiter, the head god, used his powers to reveal Rome's future greatness to Venus, who worried that this destiny might not be fulfilled:

> I shall turn forward far the hidden pages of fate and speak of the future. He [Aeneas] shall conduct a great campaign for you and conquer all Italy and its haughty peoples. . . . But his son Ascanius . . . is he who shall consolidate your power . . . [and] move his capital from Lavinium to Alba Longa, which he shall fortify to the utmost, and there a line of kings . . . shall reign. . . . And one of these, Romulus, . . . shall rule and found a city for Mars, a new city, and call his people Romans, after his name. For them I see no measure nor date, I grant them dominion [ruling power] without end . . . the master-race, the wearers of the Toga. So it is willed.[10]

The Roman Republic

For Octavian and his fellow countrymen, the idea that Rome's future greatness was willed by the gods was an article of faith. What has been actually documented by modern researchers is that by the time of the legendary founding date a town made up of crude stone and wooden huts existed on the seven Roman hills. Its inhabitants were uncultured farmers at first, but a few became wealthy as they tapped into the lucrative trade routes that wound through the foothills of the Apennines, the rugged mountains running north to south through Italy. From this landed aristocracy descended the noble patrician class.

Not much is known about Rome's early government except that it was ruled by kings, who were advised by a panel of leading patricians known as *senatores*. These city elders, or "fathers," held no real power until they threw out the last Roman king about the year 509 B.C. and established the Roman Republic, a representative government in which power rested in the hands of the Roman people, at least in theory. In practice, only citizens could vote or hold public office and only a small minority of the population—free adult males who owned weapons (which were very expensive at the time)—were eligible for citizenship. The citizens gathered periodically in a sort of town meeting called the Centuriate Assembly, which discussed and voted on important issues and formulated laws. The Assembly also elected two consuls each year to supervise government administration at home and to lead Rome's armies abroad.

The other major organ of government was the Senate, which took its name from the old-style patrician *senatores*, or senators, who composed its membership. According to Chester Starr:

> Theoretically the Senate was an advisory body, which met only when summoned by a consul or praetor [senior judge and high administrator], but the senators usually served for life and were ex-magistrates [consuls, praetors, and other officials]. Accordingly, they constituted a very important body of experienced aristocrats, normally about 300 in number. The Senate had control over the public finances and a major voice in foreign policy; as Roman power expanded overseas, the Senate also supervised the administration of the provinces.[11]

Because the senators directly advised the consuls and, through the use of wealth and high position, indirectly influenced the way members of the Assembly voted, the Senate was the real power in Rome. This made the republic an oligarchy, a government run by a powerful few, rather than a democracy.

However, the common people were not completely powerless before the senators' enormous political clout. In time, the poorer but more numerous commoners—the plebeians, or plebs—gained the right to have their own legislature, the Popular (or Tribal) Assembly. They then began annually electing ten officials, called tribunes, to look after their interests. Concerning these unique public servants, Starr writes:

> Initially the tribunes protected their fellow plebeians in matters of taxes and the draft [call-up for military service], but eventually they claimed and

A view from one wing of the interior of the Roman Senate House, where the Roman Republic's most respected and powerful politicians met regularly to decide the country's fate.

won the right to say "Veto!" (I forbid) against any unjust action of the government within the city of Rome. This was very much as if trade union leaders won the right in a modern state to veto any action they considered improper; but the plebeians backed their tribunes and protected them from patrician violence. . . . A tribune was considered sacrosanct [secure from assault], that is, anyone interfering with a tribune or injuring him was made an outlaw.[12]

Tribunician power became an extremely potent tool that everyday Romans used to check and balance the occasional abuses of authority by the aristocratic consuls and senators. Octavian would eventually take full advantage of this tool, using it in a novel way to increase his own power and prestige.

The Daunting Task of Empire

At first, the republic's complex interaction of legislative bodies, elected officials, and legal checks and balances proved flexible, strong, and for the most part capable of meeting the needs of the Roman people. The Romans therefore came to view their system with intense pride and patriotism. Such feelings, combined with the belief that they had a divine destiny to rule others, motivated the Romans to begin expanding outward from the Latium plain in the fifth century B.C. Among the neighboring Italian peoples they conquered were the more culturally advanced Etruscans, who lived north of Latium, and the warlike Samnites of south-central Italy. By about 290, Rome controlled all of central Italy. Thus began Rome's seemingly relentless policy of imperialism, the drive to expand its power and influence by dominating other lands and peoples.

Almost immediately, the Romans set their sights on the numerous Greek cities that had sprung up across southern Italy in the preceding few centuries. Some of these cities were larger and all were more culturally advanced than Rome, which was still a relatively small, dirty, and uncultured city. But the Italian Greeks had trouble uniting and their armies were smaller and much less effective than Rome's. By 265, the Romans had taken over the Greek lands and become the masters of all Italy south of the Po Valley, the northern region bordering the Italian Alps.

This marked only the beginning of Roman expansion. In the century or so that followed, Rome burst outward from the confines of its Italian homeland and involved itself in new and larger wars and conquests. After crushing Carthage in the three so-called Punic Wars, the Romans gained control of the entire western Mediterranean sphere. They then turned eastward and subdued the Greek kingdoms of the sea's eastern sphere, including Macedonia, Seleucia, and Egypt. By the end of the second century B.C. the Mediterranean had become, in effect, a

In the finale of the Third Punic War, the Romans lay siege to Carthage, the great and prosperous trading city that had once controlled the entire western Mediterranean sphere.

Roman lake. In fact, the Romans thereafter arrogantly referred to that waterway as *mare nostrum*, "our sea."

But as the crucial first century B.C. dawned, ominous cracks began to appear in the structure of Rome's republican system. That system had originally been designed to run a single city-state, one whose population shared the same language, culture, and beliefs. The Roman government was simply inadequate for the daunting task of administering a huge empire composed of dozens of diverse foreign peoples. As historian John Buchan points out:

> The new empire had grown too big and too difficult for the old machine. . . . No serious mechanism of provincial government [system of running the provinces] had been evolved. There was no permanent civil service. The governors were changed annually, and it depended wholly on their individual characters whether their terms of office were equitable or oppressive. . . . There was inadequate control by the Senate. . . . Slowly it was realized that the necessary reforms [needed to hold the empire together] could only come from the quarter where the true power now resided—the High Command, the individual who had been given overriding authority and had an army behind him.[13]

In a way, the government had left itself wide open to the challenges of powerful generals. One of its biggest mistakes had been its failure to supply retiring soldiers with adequate pensions of money and land. This left the way clear for ambitious, powerful, and wealthy adventurers to supply those pensions and thereby to win the soldiers' allegiance. Buchan continues:

> [The fortunes of the soldiers] were now linked with those of their commander; he alone could procure [get] them their due reward, and their loyalty was owed to him rather than to the state. A popular general who could raise men and attract their allegiance had a weapon so potent that it wholly upset the balance of the constitution [republican system]. Rome had no standing army in Italy and only small forces in the provinces; when an emergency came an army had to be improvised; only a general of repute could get recruits, and for that service he could make his own terms. The Senate had no hold upon an army's loyalty.[14]

A Dangerous Precedent

Thus, Octavian was born into an increasingly unstable political era in which the state struggled to maintain its authority against the challenges of ambitious military strongmen. A bloody civil war had erupted in the 80s B.C. between the forces of two such men, Gaius Marius and Cornelius Sulla. After seizing control of the capital, intimidating the Senate, and murdering thousands of his enemies, Sulla declared himself dictator. When he died suddenly in 78, the Senate managed to regain control and to reverse most of his abusive policies, but a dangerous precedent had been set, an example others would soon imitate.

The young Octavian witnessed a new challenge to republican authority by three bold and influential men. One was his great-uncle Caesar. The others were Gnaeus Pompey, a general who had be-

Marius's Reforms

"It was Marius who introduced the personal army as a decisive factor in Roman politics. Before his day the Roman soldier had in general been recruited from the small landholders of Roman territory, but the normal levies failed after the supply of these landholders had been depleted by Rome's long and costly wars. To find the troops he needed . . . Marius turned for recruits to the landless poor, the proletariat [laboring class] of Rome and the Italian [townships]. He raised an army of soldiers ready to serve under him in the hope of personal gain, that is, the acquisition of a land bonus. During the war with the Cimbri and Teutones [German tribes he defeated in 105 B.C.] . . . the number of his soldiers grew steadily. When in 100 B.C. he was consul for the sixth time, Marius had a large band of trained soldiers and veterans who owed allegiance to him and looked to him for rewards."

This drawing depicts a statue of Marius as an older man, years after he instituted profound changes in Roman military structure and methods.

come a national hero fighting pirates and rebellious slaves in the preceding decade, and Marcus Crassus, the wealthiest financier in Rome. Around 60 B.C. the three formed an unofficial but very powerful partnership that later came to be known as the First Triumvirate. Their aim was to pool their resources, since at the time none of the three possessed the power to challenge the government alone. For the next several years, the triumvirs used their combined financial, political, and military assets to intimidate the Senate and to dominate both the capital and the empire.

But the triumvirate, unable to contain the individual arrogance and ambitions of its members, eventually fell to pieces. In the 50s, Crassus died and Caesar gained untold power and prestige by conquering the rural lands and peoples of Transalpine Gaul, the area now encompassed by France and Belgium. Caesar's and Pompey's forces then faced off in a new, devastating civil war that engulfed the Roman world from Spain in the west to Egypt in the east. Caesar soundly defeated Pompey and in 45 returned to Rome as its undisputed master.

Caesar had big plans for Rome. He wanted to rebuild and beautify much of the capital, to bring prosperity to all Romans regardless of social class, and to expand Roman power and influence abroad. He knew, as many others did, that the republic could no longer govern effectively and that only a single strong individual could provide the unifying authority needed to make the system work.

A bust of Gnaeus Pompey, one of the Roman Republic's finest and most renowned generals.

A likeness of Cornelius Sulla, who declared himself dictator of Rome after defeating the forces of his rival, Marius.

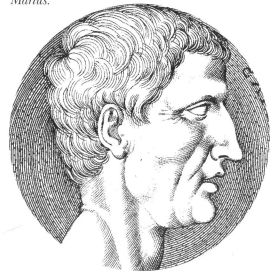

But Caesar's fatal mistake was to step outside of the old system, seemingly to trample upon custom and tradition, and to declare himself dictator for life. It began to look as if he might go still further and declare himself king. "His person was declared sacred and inviolable [untouchable]," wrote the Roman historian Appian:

> It was agreed that he should transact business on a throne of ivory and gold; that he should himself sacrifice always in triumphal costume . . . that every five years priests . . . should offer up public prayers for his safety; and that the magistrates immediately upon their inauguration should take an oath not to oppose any of Caesar's decrees.[15]

The Romans heartily despised the concept of monarchy; within the year a group of

Sulla's Lists of the Condemned

In this excerpt from the Life of Sulla, *quoted in* Plutarch: Fall of the Roman Republic, *the ancient Greek/ Roman writer Plutarch described Cornelius Sulla's merciless purge of his political opponents during the civil unrest of the 80s* B.C.

"Sulla now devoted himself entirely to the work of butchery. The city was filled with murder and there was no counting the executions or setting a limit to them. Many people were killed because of purely personal ill feeling; they had no connection with Sulla in any way, but Sulla, in order to gratify members of his own party, permitted them to be done away with. . . . Then immediately . . . Sulla published a list of eighty men to be condemned. Public opinion was horrified, but, after a single day's interval, he published another list containing 220 more names, and next day a third list with the same number of names on it. . . . He also condemned anyone who sheltered or attempted to save a person whose name was on the lists. Death was the penalty for such acts of humanity."

Sulla's list of proscribed enemies hangs in Rome's main forum. He killed and seized the property of forty senators and more than sixteen hundred other well-to-do Romans.

desperate senators formed a conspiracy. On March 15, 44 B.C., hoping to restore their beloved republic, they stabbed Caesar to death in the Senate.

Octavian Plays the Game Long

This event and the turbulent ones that followed profoundly changed the course of Ocatvian's life, for he suddenly found himself thrust into the political limelight as a participant in the power struggle that erupted after Caesar's death. At the age of nineteen, Octavian, whom Caesar had legally adopted as his son, traveled to Rome to collect his inheritance. At first he met scorn and resistance from Mark Antony, Caesar's chief military associate, now serving as one of Rome's consuls. But the shrewd Octavian, having learned a valuable lesson from his illustrious relative, quickly gained the backing of Caesar's troops and forced the much surprised and unprepared Antony to flee the city.

Octavian soon took another lesson from the dead Caesar. The young man realized that Antony would certainly raise his own army to oppose Octavian's and that other powerful generals, the strongest being Marcus Lepidus, would also challenge him for pieces of the Roman pie. As historian Donald Earl points out, Octavian knew that "he was no match for the combined armies of Antony and Lepidus."

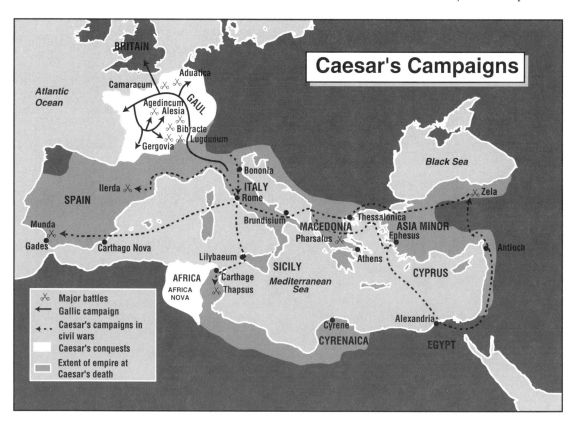

The conspirators, including the senators Brutus, Cassius, and Casca, savagely stab at Caesar, who lies dying on the blood-spattered floor of the Senate House.

And so, partly to gain recognition as their equal, in the winter of 43 B.C. Octavian boldly approached these men and suggested forming a new triumvirate. "As usual," Earl adds, Octavian "played the game [of power] long. He could afford to. He was not yet twenty years old."[16] According to historian John B. Firth in his biography of Octavian/Augustus:

> A conference was arranged to take place on a little island [in a river in northern Italy]. . . . For three days the conference lasted, and it was then announced to the expectant armies that their leaders had formed themselves into a triumvirate for the reconstitution of the state. They were to be appointed for five years with full powers to select [state officials]. . . . The provinces were to be divided into three spheres of influence . . . in which each should be supreme and secure from the meddling of his colleagues. . . . Italy was to remain neutral ground. . . . During their sinister deliberations . . . the triumvirs had decreed

not only the subversion of the republic but the ruin of their private enemies. They had determined to kill off their principal [opponents] and to safeguard their position by a massacre. The evil precedents which Marius and Sulla had established were to be followed again.[17]

After thus butchering and eliminating their main opponents, including the most influential and respected senator, Marcus Tullius Cicero, the triumvirs dealt with Caesar's assassins. Led by the popular senators Brutus and Cassius, the surviving conspirators had fled to Greece. There, they had raised a large army with which they hoped to defeat Octavian and his partners and thereby reinstate the Senate's integrity and authority. But this was a vain hope. In October 42 B.C. Antony and Octavian smashed these last republican forces on the plain of Philippi in northern Greece. Distraught and humiliated, Brutus and Cassius committed suicide; with them died the last chance of restoring the republic. Octavian would later record

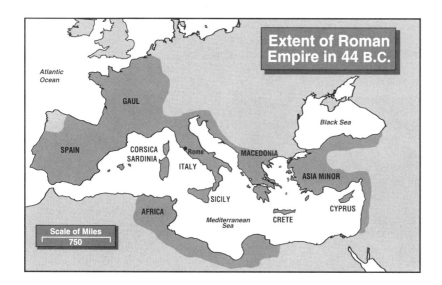

Extent of Roman Empire in 44 B.C.

these events in deceptively simple and matter-of-fact prose in the *Res gestae*: "Those who assassinated my father [Caesar] I drove into exile, avenging their crime by due process of law; and afterwards when they waged war against the state, I conquered them twice on the battlefield."[18]

The Vision, the Will, and the Power

Octavian's battles were not over, however. In the 30s B.C. history seemed to repeat itself as the Second Triumvirate, like the first such alliance, fell apart. First Octavian and Antony pushed the weaker Lepidus aside. Then they faced off in yet another round of civil strife. This time it was Octavian defending Italy and Rome's western territories against Antony, who held sway over the Roman lands and troops of the eastern Mediterranean. Supporting Antony in his bid for ultimate power was his lover, Cleopatra VII, queen of Egypt,

who threw her country's vast resources of money and grain behind the effort.

But though their forces were formidable, the lovers had met their match in

Marcus Brutus, one of the ringleaders of the conspiracy against Caesar, paid for his crime when he was defeated by Antony and Octavian on the bloody field of Philippi.

Mark Antony (left) and his lover and ally, Cleopatra VII, queen of Egypt. They gambled their vast financial and military resources against those of Octavian and lost.

Octavian. "In the jungle of Roman power-politics," Donald Dudley remarks,

> survival depended on personal quali-ties. The political gifts of Octavian were of a very high order. He could appraise a political situation with the cool judgment that Caesar had brought to military affairs. . . . Above all, he had what Caesar lacked, an acute sense of the emotive power of words, titles, and slogans. It was this that made him such a master of propa-ganda.[19]

This young master's clever and effective propaganda machine painted Cleopatra as a deceitful, scheming witch who wanted to become queen over the Romans. Antony was pictured as a weak, deluded individual who had allowed his lover to dupe him into betraying his country. The lovers countered with their own, less successful, propaganda campaign, which depicted them as the parents of a new leader men-tioned in ancient prophecy, a messiah des-tined to rule over a new and better Roman world.

Eventually this war of words turned into one of soldiers and weapons. Aided by his friend, the gifted military leader Marcus Agrippa, Octavian defeated Antony and Cleopatra at Actium, in west-ern Greece, on September 2, 31 B.C. Dur-ing this massive sea battle, which at last marked the end of Rome's destructive cy-cle of civil wars, the lovers fled and sailed back to Alexandria, the Egyptian capital. When Octavian pursued them there the following year, they killed themselves rather than surrender to his authority.

These events left Octavian, now thirty-two, the most powerful figure in the Roman world. Like his adoptive father, he wanted to use that power to bring about constructive and lasting change, an endeavor that would require significantly restructuring Rome's old government. Octavian knew full well that instituting such drastic change while maintaining his absolute authority would not be an easy task. He would have to learn to wield great power without appearing to be too ambitious, a political reality that Caesar had learned the hard way.

But the cool and calculating Octavian had the rare ability to learn from others' mistakes as well as his own and would be careful not to repeat Caesar's errors. He would attempt to capitalize on the victory at Actium, to make it one of history's deci-

The sea near the western coast of Greece is choked with warships during the massive naval encounter at Actium on September 2, 31 B.C.

"With a Spot I Damn Him"

In this excerpt from Act 4, scene 1 of Julius Caesar, *written in 1599, William Shakespeare depicts the brutal manner in which the triumvirs planned the massacre of their political opponents.*

ANTONY. These many, then, shall die; their names are pricked [written down].

OCTAVIAN. Your brother too must die. Consent you, Lepidus?

LEPIDUS. I do consent.

OCTAVIAN. Prick him down, Antony.

LEPIDUS. On condition Publius shall not live, who is your sister's son, Mark Antony.

ANTONY. He shall not live. Look, with a spot [of ink] I damn him.

sive turning points—the prelude to a dramatic new world order. So gigantic, formidable, and momentous a task would surely have frightened and ultimately defeated any ordinary individual. But the young man who had taken control of the Roman world was far from ordinary. "Behind the cold front of Octavian," John Buchan writes, "lay the vision, the will, and the power."[20]

Chapter

2 Rescuing an Upside-Down Age: The Bold New Augustan Order

Early in 29 B.C. Octavian officially concluded the civil war by directly annexing Egypt as a Roman province. This act not only ensured that no Egyptian ruler would ever again challenge Rome, but also gave Octavian, as Rome's new master, direct control over Egypt's royal treasury and huge grain supplies. He then returned to Rome in August of that year to prepare for his triumphs, the magnificent parades that would honor his victory over Antony and Cleopatra.

A few days before the first of these triumphs, Octavian enjoyed a private reading of the *Georgics*. These poems celebrating pastoral life had recently been completed by his friend Virgil. The first section contained a brief but moving prayer asking the gods to preserve the life of the man who appeared to be the war-weary Roman world's only hope for peace:

> Gods of our fathers, native gods, Romulus and our mother Vesta, you who guard the Tuscan Tiber [River] and the Palatine [Hill] of Rome, at least do not prevent this young man from the rescue of an age turned upside down.[21]

Virgil's words faithfully captured the feelings of most of his fellow Romans. Tired of the suffering, destruction, and uncertainty the many years of civil strife had brought, they longed for peace and the prosperity and happiness it promised.

To gain that peace, they were now willing to follow the lead of one powerful individual, as long as he was capable, fair, and loyal to Rome and its cherished ideals. Antony and others had shown themselves to be poor leaders as well as traitors to their country. On the other hand, Octavian, thanks in large degree to the power of his propaganda, had emerged from the war as a patriot, a skilled leader, a champion of the people, and a bringer of peace. And the people readily embraced this compelling public image. According to the Roman historian Dio Cassius in his *Roman History*:

> The Romans . . . passed many resolutions in honor of Octavian. . . . I need not record the details of the prayers, the effigies [paintings and statues of him] . . . and all the other distinctions of this kind. At first the Romans not only voted these honors, but also removed or obliterated all the monuments which commemorated Antony [and] pronounced the day of his birth accursed. . . . They then voted Octavian many more crowns and ceremonies of thanksgiving.[22]

Octavian/Augustus wears a laurel wreath and holds an eagle-topped scepter, both symbols of victory and honor.

The Only Alternative to Anarchy

It is likely that Octavian did indeed have a personal vision, at least a rough one, for a new political order. To develop and perfect his ideas, he turned to his two closest friends and associates, both of whom he had known since boyhood. One was Marcus Agrippa, the architect of Octavian's recent military victories, and the other Gaius Maecenas, a wealthy diplomat and art patron whose opinions Octavian respected. The liberal-thinking Agrippa advised the institution of an open democracy similar to those that had once existed in Athens and other Greek city-states.

However, Maecenas firmly disagreed with this idea. He pointed out that a democracy, even a highly modified one like the old Roman Republic, would not be strong or disciplined enough to administer such a large and diverse empire. "The proof of my words," he counseled Octavian (according to Dio),

> is the . . . long period during which we have engaged in civil wars and civil strife. The cause is the immense size of our population and the magnitude of the issues at stake. Our population embraces every variety of mankind in terms both of race and of character; hence both their tempers and their desires are infinitely diverse, and these evils have gone so far that they can only be controlled with great difficulty.[23]

Maecenas urged the approach Octavian was already considering. Essentially, it was the same one his great-uncle Caesar had envisioned: to institute an autocratic form of government, the kind of strong and

Through these and other honors, a majority of the Roman people expressed both their gratitude to Octavian for restoring order and their belief that he had the will and the vision to create a more constructive and harmonious age.

ordered system that seemed to be Rome's only hope of avoiding chaos. Agreeing with Maecenas, explains John Buchan, Octavian reasoned that

> law and order must be restored. The empire must be governed, and there

must be a center of power. The Roman world required a single administrative system. This could not be given by the people, for a mob could not govern. It could not be given by the Senate, which had shown itself in the highest

Agrippa Defends Democracy

According to Dio Cassius in his Roman History, *one of the most important ancient sources describing Augustus's reign, Octavian followed Gaius Maecenas's advice to establish a benign dictatorship. In doing so, he rejected Marcus Agrippa's advice to institute democracy. Supposedly, Agrippa told Octavian:*

A bust of Marcus Agrippa, Augustus's friend, military strategist, and personal adviser. Agrippa was a far-sighted thinker who recognized the political potential of democracy.

"The fact that . . . democracies are greatly superior to monarchies, is shown by the example of Greece [specifically, Athens and a few other city-states during the period of 500 to 300 B.C.]. So long as the peoples of Greece were subject to monarchies, they achieved nothing of consequence, but once they began to live under popular rule, their fame spread throughout the world. . . . But why need we refer to the examples set by other peoples, when we have our own at home? We Romans at first lived under a different form of government [a kingship]. Then, after enduring many harsh experiences, we longed to obtain our liberty. After we had won it, we rose to the position of proud authority which we enjoy today. . . . At any rate, the ancient Romans hated tyranny so passionately . . . that they even declared that form of government [monarchy] to be accursed."

degree incompetent, and in any case had no means of holding the soldiers' loyalty. Only . . . a man who had the undivided allegiance of [the] army . . . must be the master of the state. The idea of a personal sovereign [monarch], which had come from . . . the east, and had long been hovering at the back of Roman minds, must now become a fact, for it was the only alternative to anarchy.[24]

"Show No Arrogance and Take No Advantage"

But Octavian realized that successfully leading Rome into this brave new world of one-man rule would be difficult and tricky. While the Roman people were ready for substantial change, they still respected and clung to ancient traditions, including many political ones. In other words, they wanted a new approach to the future but at the same time stubbornly desired to maintain some kind of continuity with their past. And though they might accept some kind of one-man rule, they still deeply despised the concept of kingship and would surely reject any man who claimed that title. Octavian's great challenge, then, was to hold on to the autocratic power he had won for himself without scrapping the old system. And most importantly, he must do this without calling himself a king or an emperor, or projecting the image of such a ruler in any way.

Here, Maecenas's advice was once more instrumental. He suggested that Octavian should create for himself the image of a simple man of the people, a fair leader who respected the law, tradition, and religion, and whose main aim was to bring prosperity and happiness to his people. Said Maecenas:

> If you perform of your own accord all the actions which you would wish another man to perform if he were your ruler, you will . . . succeed in all your endeavors and . . . lead a life . . . free from danger. For how can men fail to regard you with affection as their father and their savior, when they see that you are both disciplined and principled in your life, formidable in war and yet disposed to peace, that you show no arrogance and take no advantage . . . [and] do not live in luxury while imposing hardships on others. . . . You hold in your hands the most potent guarantee of your security—the fact that you never do wrong to another.[25]

With Maecenas's advice in mind, Octavian eventually decided that the solution to the political challenge he faced was to assume a broad range of powers, all legal within and officially blessed by the traditional republican system. He would, writes John Firth, attempt to "retain the semblance of a republic, the semblance of liberty and freedom, and the semblance of the old constitution." Yet at the same time he would retain his absolute political and military power. In this way he would shift the basis of state power away from the Senate and the people to himself, while keeping the legislatures, officials, and other outward trappings of the old republican system. In practice, he would acquire for himself the powers of these institutions and officials without assuming their titles, and also without taking the title of king. "An organized hypocrisy [false appearance], perhaps," comments Firth, "but one which fully served its purpose and helped to smooth the transition from the old to the new."[26]

The Slate Wiped Clean

Octavian heralded the coming of the new order by two dramatic public acts. The first occurred in 29 B.C. during his victory triumphs, which wound through the streets of Rome, past the Capitoline Hill with its sacred shrines to Jupiter, and into the main Forum. There, he dedicated a new temple to Minerva (equivalent of the Greek Athena), goddess of war. But it was his next move that spurred the huge crowds of onlookers to rounds of frenzied cheers and applause. Solemnly, Octavian approached the temple of Janus, the god who watched over doorways and who was associated with new beginnings. By tradition, the double gates of his temple were symbolically left open during times of war and closed when Rome's empire was at peace. Only twice before in their long history had the Romans closed these doors. Now, in a grand gesture, the victor of Actium did so, and all who bore witness realized that this act—in effect a pledge to maintain the peace—symbolized a new beginning for the nation.

Octavian's second public act was also designed to put past strife, hatreds, and bloodshed behind and to signal a fresh beginning. He certainly could not go through the fiction of restoring the republic without renouncing his own many illegal, murderous, and antirepublican acts as a triumvir. Dio wrote:

> Then, recognizing that he had caused many unjust and illegal measures to be enacted during the period of strife between political factions and the civil wars, especially at the time when Antony and Lepidus had shared the Triumvirate with him, he rescinded every one of these by means of a single decree.[27]

With this sweeping edict, issued in 28 B.C., Octavian officially annulled all the former decrees and acts of the triumvirate and thereby wiped the slate clean of any legal obstacles to the restoration of republican authority.

In the eyes of the people, these initial gestures seemed to confirm Octavian's fairness and sincerity, and his popularity continued to soar. Sensing that he had the backing of a vast majority of the citizens, he began to implement his plan for a new government. Over the next few years, he slowly and shrewdly consolidated a wide array of powers, always in what appeared to be a legal and aboveboard manner in full accordance with established Roman law and tradition. Following Maecenas's advice, he did not attempt to confer any powers or titles on himself. Indeed, he saw no need, as the senators were more than happy to do it for him. Octavian's wide popularity and apparent willingness to bring back at least a semblance of republican and senatorial authority had won him their respect and support. They now believed as he did that a benign dictator who would rule in the republic's name could bring Rome order and prosperity.

Creation of the *Principate*

The Senate made a grand show of its support for the state's new leader in a splendid ceremony held on January 16, 27 B.C. The Roman fathers thanked Octavian for "saving the country," and then presented him with a laurel wreath, a symbol of honor and glory. They also gave him a magnificent golden shield bearing an inscription proclaiming his *clementia*, or clemency, his *justitia*, or justice, and his *pietas*, or sense of duty.

Next, the senators decreed that henceforth Octavian would be called by the majestic title of Augustus. According to Dio:

> At the time when [the senators and the people] wished to give him some title of special importance . . . Octavian had set his heart strongly on being named Romulus. But when he understood that this aroused suspicions that he desired the kingship [because Romulus had been Rome's first king], he abandoned his efforts to obtain it and adopted the title of Augustus, as signifying that he was something more than human, since indeed all the most precious and sacred objects are referred to as *augusta*.[28]

In honor of the leader and his new name, the Senate officially changed the month known as *Sextilis* to Augustus (now August).[29] The new title of Augustus was added to Octavian's family name of Caesar. Because of Julius Caesar's larger-than-life image, that name already had a magical, almost superhuman significance, which would later be perpetuated as Augustus's heirs used the name Caesar as a title of lofty authority.

Another important title Augustus already held was that of *imperator*, or supreme commander. By tradition, a general had the right to receive this title from his troops after scoring a military victory. Although he was bound to give up the title when he entered the borders of the capital, thereby acknowledging his subservience to the state, he could reclaim it if he won another victory. In 43 B.C., Octavian's troops, or more precisely Caesar's veterans who had recently thrown their support to the young man, had proclaimed him *imperator*. To bolster Octavian's authority during the prelude to the civil war, in 38 Agrippa had ordered coins struck bearing the younger Caesar's image and the words "Imperator Caesar, Son of the Deified Julius." Now, in 27, though Augustus clearly stood within Rome's borders, he was allowed to break with tradition and to keep this title permanently. Thus, his full official name became Imperator Augustus Caesar.

In time, because he had created a long-lasting position of absolute power, the term *imperator* would evolve into the word *emperor*. But in his own lifetime Augustus was always careful to avoid being called emperor, lord, "your highness," or any other title suggestive of kingship. He preferred instead the unofficial and more modest name of *princeps*, meaning "first citizen." This gave the impression that he considered himself to be no better than the average Roman. And he bolstered his image as a simple man of the people in another way. Heeding Maecenas's warning not to live in luxury while his people suffered hardship, Augustus and his wife, Livia, thereafter lived in a small, modestly

A silver denarius, minted during Augustus's reign, bears his image. He took control of and supervised the imperial coin mints and standardized the monetary system, giving all coins a fixed value.

furnished house and rejected the usual lavish lifestyle of the wealthy and powerful.

Augustus's speech to the senators acknowledging the honors they had bestowed on him reflected this new image of extreme modesty and sincerity. According to Suetonius, he declared:

> May I be privileged to build firm and lasting foundations for the Government of the State. May I also achieve the reward to which I aspire: that of being known as the author of the best possible Constitution, and of carrying with me, when I die, the hope that these foundations which I have established for the State will abide secure.[30]

Just how much of this new benign image was sincere and how much a political ploy will never be known. What is certain is that, despite calling himself *princeps*, in reality Augustus was an absolute monarch. And what, according to law, constituted his "term of service" must more accurately be described as an emperor's reign. Ironi-cally, the term that came to denote that long reign and its government—the *Principate*, which began on that January day in 27 B.C.—was derived from the word *princeps*.

The Pillars of Authority

In the initial months and years of the *Principate*, Augustus continued to increase his prestige and broaden his powers. He exercised complete control over Egypt, Gaul, Cilicia in Asia Minor, and several other provinces that, because of their wealth of natural resources and/or strategic military value, were considered key imperial territories. This limited the Senate's administrative powers to Italy and the less strategic provinces. Augustus also gained the right to declare war or peace without consulting the Senate, a privilege no consul had ever enjoyed. Regarding the consulship itself, the yearly elections of two consuls continued as usual. However, the *princeps* now held permanent authority equal to that of these leaders, which in effect made him a third consul, though without the title. This gave him the legal right to conduct state foreign policy.

Perhaps the most potent political advantage Augustus acquired involved the tribunate, the office held by the tribunes. The tribunician powers to veto laws, to defend citizens' rights, and to arrest corrupt officials, even consuls, were both sweeping and formidable. Once again, the challenge for Augustus was his need to maintain the appearance of respecting tradition. He was a patrician, and by law only a plebeian could become a tribune.

The solution, as in the case of his permanent consular powers, was for the Senate and the Tribal Assembly to make a special arrangement that applied only to Augustus. The idea was to give him what amounted to tribunician powers without going against ancient tradition by granting him either the office or title of tribune. Thus, Henry Rowell explains, in 23 B.C.,

> Augustus received from the Roman people all the rights and powers inherent in the tribunate for life, without becoming a tribune. . . . In the Senate he could initiate or veto decrees, and he could also preside over the Tribal Assembly. . . . His person had already been made sacrosanct, and he had been granted the right to protect his fellow citizens. But possibly of greater importance than these legal consequences of the [tribunician] power was the psychological effect upon the people of Rome. By accepting this new kind of tribunate for life, Augustus had proclaimed himself the champion of the interests of the people, the protector of the weak and humble.[31]

Indeed, considering their broad range and high degree of prestige, his special tribunician powers constituted one of the two strongest pillars supporting his authority. As John Buchan puts it, "The *Principate* was not a dictatorship or a kingship or a more potent consulship, but a magnified tribuneship."[32]

The other major pillar of Augustus's power was the Roman army. Soon after initiating the *Principate*, he drastically reduced the size of the army from almost seventy legions, or regiments of about 5,000 men each, to twenty-eight, a total of slightly more than 150,000 men. He did this for both financial and security reasons. Maintaining a larger army during peacetime would have drained both the state treasury and his own pockets and at the same time put a huge strain on the empire's food production capacity. As historian Michael Grant points out in *The Army of the Caesars*, a bigger army would also

> have been a perilous security risk. After all, Augustus was in a better position than anyone else to know how large an army in the empire as a whole, and how large a garrison in each individual province, he could command without offering a potential prey to Roman military rebels.[33]

The *imperator* also instituted several important military reforms. All of these were designed to increase the army's efficiency and also to eliminate the problem that had brought the republic to its knees—troops swearing loyalty to individual generals rather than to the state. He banned conscription, the military draft, except in the case of national emergency, and opted instead for a professional standing army of volunteers. He reasoned that career

Army Salaries and Bonuses

In his detailed, insightful study of the evolution of the Roman army, The Army of the Caesars, *historian Michael Grant makes these points about the pay the soldiers, called legionnaires, received under Augustus.*

"The basic [annual] rate of legionnaires' pay, which [Julius] Caesar had raised to 225 *denarii*, remained unchanged. For Augustus did not deem it either desirable or economically practical to effect a further increase. Nor can the rate have been intolerably low, since it still stayed the same for eighty years after Augustus's death. And, although there were inevitably complaints, this total was enough . . . to enable some soldiers . . . to save nearly one-third of what they earned. . . . These wages might not have been enough to guarantee the soldiers' loyalty. What turned the scale, however, was . . . [Augustus's policy] of supplementing the soldiers' pay by special bonuses (*donativa*). . . . After [the Battle of] Actium the legionnaires who were retained in his service received bonuses, and in addition the *princeps* himself recorded [in his *Res gestae*] that he gave 120,000 legionary veterans . . . 250 *denarii* [apiece]. . . . Soldiers' pay is generally reckoned in *denarii* or *sestertii*, of which there were four [*sestertii*] to the *denarius*. . . . Under Augustus . . . the *denarius* was the standard silver coin, valued at one twenty-fifth of the standard gold coin, the *aureus*. The *sesterius* was at this period a large brass token coin. Unfortunately it is quite impossible to give any useful modern equivalents of these denominations, owing to the notorious absence of ancient economic statistics."

This raised bas-relief beautifully captures the details of Roman military uniforms.

men who enlisted by choice were more likely to support the establishment than a renegade general. Augustus also required soldiers to swear an oath to him as their supreme commander once each year. In addition, he granted them hefty bonuses and created a system of land grants as part of their pensions, making it almost impossible for a general to buy their allegiance. Augustus also created a special force of about nine thousand elite, highly paid troops, called the Praetorian Guard. Its membership was restricted to men of Italian birth and its primary task was to see that his orders and policies were enforced.

The Role of the Senate

It might seem that with Augustus holding so many diverse powers the Senate had no powers or dignity left of its own. But this was not the case. The *princeps* dominated

The soldier at left wears a lorca squamata, *a tunic of armor scales; his companion wears a* lorca segmentata, *a leather tunic with attached metal strips.*

Members of the Praetorian Guard, the elite corps of soldiers created by Augustus to ensure implementation of his policies.

that body, to be sure. He oversaw admission of new senators, had the power to expel those he deemed poor legislators, and often took part in and dominated senatorial debates. However, he recognized that he had to allow the senators a certain measure of authority and prestige, not only to keep himself from seeming too autocratic, but also to maintain its support. The Senate was, after all, the greatest symbol of Roman tradition and the central focus of Italy's political and social aristocracy. And so, under Augustus, Donald Dudley explains, the Senate

> still enjoyed [a certain degree of] prestige and powers, administering Rome, Italy and [several of] the more highly civilized provinces, serving as a high court of justice and appeal, conferring, or in theory, withholding grants of power to the *princeps* himself.[34]

Augustus also appeased the Senate by creating the *consilium*. This was a special advisory body composed of the consuls, fifteen senators chosen by lot, and a few other high officials. The *consilium* set the agenda for senatorial sessions and advised Augustus on policy matters. "He encouraged all comers to offer suggestions," wrote Dio, "in case anybody could think of some improvement [in how the government ran], and he allowed them complete freedom of speech."[35]

Yet it is important to view the republican powers and privileges held by the legislators and the people in a realistic light. While Augustus allowed the senators and the people generous civil liberties and, through the annual elections held by the assemblies, a considerable voice in choosing leaders, he remained, behind the scenes, firmly in charge of the whole show.

According to Dio, "nothing was done that did not meet with Augustus's approval."[36]

A New Branch on the Roman Tree

As the *princeps* quietly and patiently brought about his bold new political order, the war-weary Romans entered an age of peace and prosperity unlike any they had ever experienced. The safer and more comfortable their lives became, the more they saw Augustus as a man of his word and a leader to be trusted and supported. This perception motivated them to lavish even more praises and powers on him. In 12 B.C. a gigantic crowd of cheering citizens granted Augustus the post of *pontifex maximus*, chief priest of the state religion. Ten years later, the people gave him the prestigious title of *pater patriae*, or "father of his country." Though no special powers were attached to this title, it was a heartfelt expression of the respect, love, and sense of duty the people felt for him. Supposedly, when a delegation of citizens informed him of the honor, he cried openly and said, "I have at last achieved my highest ambition. What more can I ask of the immortal gods than that they may permit me to enjoy your approval until my dying day?"[37]

Though the *princeps* may well have sincerely cherished public approval, it was hardly his highest ambition. His singular dream was undoubtedly to build a new and more efficient Roman system using the best pieces of the wreckage of the old one. "His great aim," writes Firth, "was to graft the *Principate* upon the Republic. He did not wish to uproot the old tree and

Father of His Country

In this excerpt from his Lives of the Twelve Caesars, *Suetonius described how the Romans, grateful to Augustus for bringing them peace and prosperity, honored him with the title of* pater patriae.

"In a universal movement to confer on Augustus the title 'Father of His Country,' the first approach was made by the commons [members of the Tribal Assembly], who sent a deputation [delegation] to him. . . . When he declined this honor a huge crowd met him outside the Theater with laurel wreaths, and repeated the request. Finally, the Senate followed suit . . . [and] chose Valerius Messala to speak for them all. . . . Messala's words were: 'Caesar Augustus, I am instructed to wish you and your family good fortune and divine blessings; which amounts to wishing that our entire State will be fortunate and our country prosperous. The Senate agrees with the people of Rome in saluting you as Father of Your Country.' With tears in his eyes, Augustus answered—again I quote his exact words: 'Fathers of the Senate, I have at last achieved my highest ambition. What more can I ask of the immortal gods than that they may permit me to enjoy your approval until my dying day?'"

plant a new one; his desire was to furnish the old tree with a new branch, which should be the most vital of all its limbs."[38]

Augustus himself was that new branch, the benign dictator who genuinely believed he alone knew what was best for the country. Through the wise and restrained use of overwhelming power, he achieved his aim. And the result was a new, richly diverse, immensely powerful, and decidedly autocratic political entity thereafter known as the Roman Empire. To many who lived at the height of the Augustan Age, it seemed as though Jupiter's promise to grant Rome "dominion without end" had been fulfilled.

3 From Town of Bricks to City of Marble: Transforming the Roman Capital

Having legally consolidated so many offices and institutions under his personal control, Rome's *princeps* possessed an enormous amount of power at his fingertips. Finding themselves in a similar position, many other national leaders before and after him abused their power by selfishly indulging their own pleasures or engaging in aggressive, warlike behavior. But to Augustus's credit, for the most part he used his great powers for more constructive and creative purposes. And the concept of positive reform—of healing the nation's wounds, of building anew, and of restoring lost values—became the hallmark of his long reign.

This policy of building something new and better on the ruins of the past was most evident in Augustus's impressive public building programs. At the beginning of his reign, Rome was already a large, populous, and important city. But it was old, dirty, chaotic, unattractive, and suffered regularly from such disasters as floods, fires that consumed whole districts, and poorly constructed apartment buildings that collapsed, killing and maiming many. In Augustus's view, this was hardly a fitting centerpiece for his new imperial order. The Roman Empire needed a capital that would stand as an example of the wealth, nobility, civility, and all the other "superior" qualities of the Mediterranean's so-called master race. At Augustus's direction, therefore, the city of Rome underwent a mighty burst of urban renewal and large-scale municipal reorganization. As Suetonius summed it up:

> Aware that the city was architecturally unworthy of her position as capital of the Roman Empire, besides being vulnerable to fire and river floods, Augustus so improved her appearance that he could justifiably boast: "I found Rome built of bricks; I leave her clothed in marble." He also used as much foresight as could have possibly been provided in guarding against future disasters.[39]

A Miserable and Unsafe City

The great extent of Augustus's rebuilding programs becomes clear when one considers what the city of Rome was like before his reforms. Like Athens and most other cities of the day, Rome was already many centuries old. Its streets, originally meandering footpaths and trails, were laid out in a haphazard fashion, and whole blocks of buildings had been built, rebuilt, and rebuilt again on the ruins of older structures. In 27 B.C., when Octavian was preparing to receive his new name of Augustus, the historian Livy, who was then compiling his great history of Rome, wrote: "The old sewers which were originally laid down in public property now pass here and there under private houses and the [present] form of the city resembles more a squatters' settlement than a planned community."[40]

Overpopulation, or perhaps more accurately overcrowding, was certainly a major factor contributing to the overall confusion, filth, and squalor of the city. By the late first century B.C. Rome had probably close to one million inhabitants, most of them crammed within a central area of only a few dozen square miles. Lack of space forced builders to a vertical solution; that is, adding more and more stories to existing structures, especially

Merchants, shoppers, soldiers, and slaves swarm through one of Rome's narrow streets. The first-century A.D. poet Juvenal colorfully described such city crowds in his Satires.

residential apartment buildings. In a famous essay on ancient Greek and Roman architecture, *De architectura*, the Roman architect Vitruvius commented about these aspects of pre-Augustan Rome:

> The majesty [fame and allure] of the city and the considerable increase in its population have compelled an extraordinary extension of the dwelling houses, and circumstances have constrained [forced] men to take refuge in increasing the height of the edifices.[41]

Many of the tenement buildings were five, six, or more stories high and most were poorly built, which often proved disastrous for those who dwelled in them. Donald Earl explains that rich builders and building owners

> took advantage of the needs of the poor [for affordable housing] to realize maximum profits by the provision of minimum facilities. Foundations were laid in swampy ground, substandard materials were used, the principles of safe construction were ignored. Roman architects were well aware that a certain height of building demanded a certain thickness of wall. Yet many contractors ignored this . . . principle and raised apartment blocks far higher than the walls would support. . . . Another favorite device to meet and profit by the . . . demand for hous-

A City Shored Up with Props

Although Augustus's building regulations and fire brigades made living in the city much safer, poor construction and fire damage continued to plague the poorer sections of Rome for generations. In his Satires, *quoted in* The Norton Book of Classical Literature, *the poet Juvenal, who lived from ca.* A.D. *60 to ca. 130, complained:*

"What countryman ever bargained . . . for his house collapsing about his ears? . . . Here we live in a city shored up, for the most part, with cheap stays and props: that's how our landlords arrest the collapse of their property, papering over great cracks in the ramshackle fabric, reassuring the tenants they can sleep secure, when all the time the building is poised like a house of cards [ready to collapse]. I prefer to live where fires and midnight panics are not quite such common events. By the time the smoke's got up to your third-floor apartment (and you still asleep) your downstairs neighbor is roaring for water, and shifting his bits and pieces [meager belongings] to safety. If the alarm goes at ground-level, the last to fry will be the attic tenant, way up among the nesting pigeons, with nothing but tiles between himself and the weather."

ing was to add further stories to already existing buildings with foundations and walls insufficiently strong to carry the extra load. The inevitable result was the frequent collapse of apartment blocks and houses.[42]

Augustus was alarmed by such disasters. Whether his distress stemmed from a genuine concern for the plight of the impoverished plebs who lived in these death traps, or from his embarrassment that Rome's capital was miserable and unsafe to live in, remains unclear (perhaps it was a bit of both). In any case, he did pass building regulations that forbade the erection of houses and tenements more than seventy feet high. This and other similar regulations laid the foundation for the more extensive building safety code enacted by later emperors.

Rebuilding Rome's Infrastructure

The *princeps* also recognized and seriously addressed other problems that made life in Rome miserable and unsafe for rich and poor alike. For one thing, it was difficult and costly to administer and to keep in repair such a large, chaotic city. Because of lack of funds, manpower, or both, public officials often neglected the roads, both inside and outside the city limits, the many public temples and altars where the people worshiped, and the stone aqueducts that piped millions of gallons of water into the city each day. By the late 30s B.C., after decades of civil strife and mismanagement of public funds, most of these structures were crumbling.

In addition, fires periodically ravaged Rome, destroying entire sections, some of which remained piles of rubble for years and added to the rapid growth of slums. It might seem incredible that in such a huge metropolis, where oil lamps, the main source of night lighting, regularly caused fires, no effective fire-fighting force existed. Yet this was the case. Rome also had no police force, which made walking the streets at night a risky venture.

Using both public funds and often his own money, Augustus attempted to remedy all of these problems. To make the tasks of administration and upkeep easier, he divided the city into fourteen *regiones*, or districts. Each district further broke down into several *vici*, the counterpart of modern wards or precincts, of which there were more than two hundred in all. Each *vicus* had four *magistri*, local administrators who were elected annually by the people who lived in their respective wards. These elections were one way that Augustus tried to emphasize the continuity of republican institutions and to make the people feel that they had a say in how they were governed. In reality the *magistri* had little real authority and usually merely carried out the policies handed down from above, a chain of command stretching back to Augustus himself.

Through this administrative chain, Augustus oversaw widespread and impressive improvements in Rome's infrastructure, or its system of public facilities and services. Among the first facilities rebuilt were the roads, about which Dio Cassius recorded:

> Augustus had noticed that the roads . . . had been so neglected that it had become difficult to travel along them.

He therefore ordered some of the senators to have the other roads repaired at their expense, while he himself dealt with the *Via Flaminia* [the road leading from the heart of the city northward across the width of Italy].... The work was completed without delay.... The other roads were repaired later, either at public expense or at that of Augustus.[43]

The *princeps* entrusted the overhaul of the aqueducts, with their life-giving flow of fresh water, to the brilliant and energetic Agrippa, who became, in effect, Rome's first permanent water commissioner. Before Agrippa began this monumental task, four aqueducts served the city, the oldest being the Aqua Appia, built in 312 B.C. Agrippa added the Aqua Julia and the Aqua Virgo, completing the latter in 19 B.C. He also trained a special company of 240 slaves to repair, clean, and generally maintain the city's entire water system, which included miles of stone sewers, or cloacae.[44] As Henry Rowell explains, Agrippa was responsible not only for supplying water, but also for maintaining Rome's sanitation and public health:

> Only an abundance of water going beyond the normal needs of drinking, cooking, and washing could make it possible to flush away the city's refuse through the sewers. It is no coincidence that Agrippa cleaned the sewers in the year in which he built the Julian aqueduct.... Water supply and refuse disposal were closely connected.[45]

Even after Agrippa's death in 12 B.C., Augustus continued improving the water system. He appointed a water board made up of a commissioner, the *curator aquarum*, and two assistants, the *audiutores*. These officials oversaw the now experienced unit of slaves that Agrippa had previously trained.

The famed Appian Way, main artery of southern Italy, was originally built by and named for the censor Appius Claudius Caecus. It eventually stretched from Rome to Brundisium.

(Above) A reconstructed view of an aqueduct near Rome; (below) the actual remains of the aqueduct at Segovia, in Spain, which stands 128 feet high and stretches for over ten miles.

The "Watchmen" and Urban Cohorts

One of Augustus's most important improvements in Rome's infrastructure was the creation of a fire-fighting brigade. It should be noted that his first two tries were unsuccessful. In the first, in 23 B.C., he placed six hundred slaves under the direction of the aediles, public officials in charge of maintaining streets and public buildings. Finding that this arrangement did not work well, in 7 B.C. he removed these slaves to the authority of the *magistri* of the various wards. This worked no better. One reason that these early brigades proved inefficient was that they were too small to patrol such a large city; also, the slaves, who enjoyed neither freedom nor pay, had little incentive to work hard or to risk their lives to save the property of people who did enjoy these benefits.

In A.D. 6 the *princeps*, having recognized his past mistakes, set up a professional force of about seven thousand firemen called *vigiles*, or "watchmen." These were freedmen, former slaves who had gained their freedom, who were paid regular salaries. In addition to their chief duty, fighting fires, the *vigiles* had the authority to arrest thieves, muggers, and burglars and to enforce the regulation that people keep extra supplies of water in their homes and apartments in case of fire.

Though the *vigiles* were granted extra police powers, they were usually preoccupied with their main duty and so did not constitute an effective police force. According to Earl, Augustus saw a pressing need for full-time police officers, and so placed the duties of maintaining the public peace and rounding up criminals

> in the hands of three Urban Cohorts [*cohortes urbanae*], each 1,000 strong, a semi-military body under the ultimate command of the Prefect of the City [the *praefectus urbi*, an outmoded republican office that Augustus revived especially for this purpose]. In the case of serious disorder assistance could be summoned from the Praetorian Cohorts, Augustus's own guard, comprising nine infantry cohorts and a squadron of cavalry. . . . Augustus normally kept three of these cohorts in Rome and stationed the other six in various Italian towns.[46]

The High Noon of the *Principate*

While the essential improvements Augustus made in the roads, water system, and

fire and police forces were dramatic, most people at the time, both locals and foreigners alike, were far more impressed by his more outwardly showy construction of new public buildings. One of the many he later bragged about in the *Res gestae* was the new Senate House, begun by Julius Caesar to replace the old one, which had burned to the ground in 52 B.C. Augustus finished the building and dedicated it in 29 B.C. Other imposing Augustan buildings included: a temple to Apollo, god of the sun, healing, and prophecy, on the Palatine Hill; additions to the Circus Maximus, the immense stadium for chariot races begun in earlier centuries; two temples to Jupiter on the Capitoline Hill; and another temple to Jupiter, as well as temples to Minerva and Juno, Jupiter's wife and protector of women, on the Aventine Hill.

Augustus also boasted in the *Res gestae*, "On ground bought for the most part from private owners I built the theater adjoining the Temple of Apollo which was to be inscribed with the name of my son-in-law [and nephew] Marcus Marcellus."[47] The son of Augustus's sister Octavia, Marcellus died suddenly in 23 B.C. at the age of nineteen, and the *princeps*, who had been devoted to the boy, wanted to honor his memory. Completed in 11 B.C., the magnificent Theater of Marcellus had seating for fourteen thousand persons, making it the largest of Rome's three stone theaters.

The structures that most expressed the ideals of Augustus's *Principate*—the strength and grandeur of Rome, respect for ancient tradition, and the maintenance of peace—were the Augustan Forum and the *Ara Pacis*, or Altar of Peace. The centerpiece of his new Forum was the

The Theater of Marcellus

"It seated approximately 14,000, making it the largest of [Rome's] three permanent stone theaters. The reconstructed ground plan indicates that the vaulted side passageways between the stage (*pulpitum*) and the first tier of seats served as entranceways to the lower tier of seats. Above these were the *tribunalia* [seats reserved for government officials]. Other seats in the theater could be reached by the central passageway (*praecinctio*) and radiating stairways, or by stairways and tunnels under the seating areas opening into these areas by *vomitoria* [entrances]. A colonnaded gallery was located at the top of the *cavea* [seating area]. Storerooms on each side of the stage, a scene building directly behind the *scaenae frons* [wall at the rear of the stage], and a rear terrace and portico completed this theater complex."

The remains of the Theater of Marcellus, largest of Rome's stone theaters, named in honor of Augustus's beloved nephew.

An excellent reconstruction of the mammoth Circus Maximus, with the central axis, or spina, *dividing the racetrack, and the column-lined emperor's box rising in the stands at left.*

Temple of Mars the Avenger. According to Suetonius, "Augustus had vowed to build the Temple of Mars during the Philippi campaign of vengeance against Julius Caesar's assassins. He therefore decreed that the Senate should meet here whenever declarations of war . . . were considered."[48] Two grand colonnades surrounding this temple housed what amounted to a Roman hall of fame, a series of statues to the great men of Rome's past. "Next to the Immortals [the gods]," Suetonius wrote,

> Augustus most honored the memory of those citizens who had raised the Roman people from small beginnings to their present glory; which is why he . . . raised statues to them, wearing triumphal dress, in the twin colonnades of his Forum. Then he proclaimed: "This has been done to make my fellow-

citizens insist that both I . . . and my successors, shall not fall below the standard set by those great men of old."[49]

The Altar of Peace was a monument to the *Pax Augustae*, the Peace of Augustus; that is, the new period of tranquility he had "bestowed" on the Roman people by concluding the long civil wars. Its form was of a simple altar stone surrounded by a magnificently decorated band of sculptures. Describing the procession of figures depicted, Donald Dudley writes:

> It is the high noon of the *Principate*: Augustus is there with his friends Agrippa and Maecenas, [and] the younger members of the imperial family and their children. The procession moves with an easy dignity, serious but not solemn. Augustus is not put in any

central position. . . . He walks at the head of the procession among the priests and their attendants—the First Citizen, certainly, but not set apart from the Senate and the people.[50]

Encouraged by his friend the *princeps*, Agrippa also built a splendid complex of buildings, which came to dominate the large open public area known as the Campus Martius, or Field of Mars. Among these structures was a basilica to Neptune, the sea god, and a pantheon, a type of building with circular walls, in this case a temple dedicated to the Julii family, which had produced both Caesar and Augustus. According to Strabo's account, Agrippa's complex had "many colonnades in a circle around it and sacred precincts [religious areas] and . . . theaters, and an amphitheater [stadium] and opulent [richly decorated] temples, all in close succession to one another."[51]

Bread and Circuses

That Augustus sponsored and encouraged so much city renovation to impress residents of the provinces and other countries with Rome's splendor cannot be doubted. But he had another motive that was directed closer to home. This was to awe, to appease, and thereby to maintain the respect and support of the Roman people. He knew full well that if the people were unhappy and angry he would have to use the army to control them, which would be expensive and also dangerous, since it would only lead to more discontent and perhaps even open rebellion. Under such conditions, his reign would surely be miserable and unproductive. Therefore, the relentless municipal improvements he made were designed partly to build the trust and boost the morale of the people.

This first-century A.D. *terracotta plaque shows a* quadrigarum, *a four-horse chariot, speeding toward the turning posts at the end of the racetrack's* spina. *A single horseman, partially visible at right, rides ahead, setting the race's frantic pace.*

Augustus used other shrewd and effective ways to keep the masses content and busy, and therefore under control. Again, the policies of his dead great-uncle were instructive. During the civil wars, many people had lost their jobs, their farms, or found their lives otherwise disrupted, and in desperation large numbers of poor had migrated to the city. Caesar found it necessary to create a huge "corn dole," or regular free public handout of grain, to control what he and other patricians arrogantly called "the mob."

To keep this potentially dangerous mob occupied, Caesar also increased the number of annual public holidays, during which the government furnished free public entertainment, from sixty-five to seventy-six. Such entertainment included theatrical plays, gladiator and wild animal fights, and horse and chariot races in stadiums called circuses. Thus, the policy of appeasing the masses through free food and shows became known as "bread and circuses."

Augustus not only adopted this policy, he greatly expanded it. He often paid for the grain for the corn dole himself, as evidenced by his boast in the *Res gestae*: "In my eleventh consulship [23 B.C.] I made twelve distributions of food out of the grain purchased at my own expense."[52] If part of his goal was to win the people's hearts, he succeeded. His generous spon-

Gladiators engage in mortal combat in a Roman arena. Contrary to popular belief, the "thumbs-down" gesture was the spectators' signal for the victor to drop his weapon and spare his fallen opponent.

The Mighty Circus

Here, from his insightful study Rome in the Augustan Age, *classical scholar Henry T. Rowell describes how the mighty Circus Maximus, which seated more than 250,000 spectators, appeared in Augustus's reign.*

"The Circus was one of Rome's most magnificent buildings in the Augustan Age. Its very size was imposing, about two thousand feet long by three hundred feet wide. The spectators, sitting in three sections of seats which rose behind each other, were separated from the arena by a broad channel of water which protected them from the wild beasts. For although the building was primarily designed for horse and chariot racing, animal and gladiatorial shows were also held there. A wall running lengthwise divided the arena into two parts. On it Augustus placed an obelisk [tall, pointed monument] which he had imported from Heliopolis, in Egypt. . . . The building was faced with marble. It was surrounded by a colonnade, at the back of which, under the seats, were shops with living quarters above them. Between them were the entrances and staircases leading to the seats. The vicinity was a haunt [favorite area] for fortunetellers, prostitutes, and other dubious characters in search of customers in the crowd. Horace [the prominent Augustan poet] took pleasure in wandering about in this raffish [vulgar] atmosphere."

sorship of the dole headed off mass starvation during serious famines that struck in 22 B.C. and A.D. 6; not surprisingly, his popularity soared.

Enthusiastically maintaining the other half of "bread and circuses," the *princeps* added another fifteen annual holidays featuring free public entertainment. In fact, he sponsored so many races, gladiator fights, and other shows that he set a precedent that all of his successors had no choice but to follow if they wanted to keep the urban mob's allegiance. Under the frail and cultured Augustus, these enter-

tainments were rarely brutal or sadistic. To set a humane tone for the games, he forbade victorious gladiators from killing their defeated opponents. He himself preferred athletic contests to bloody fights and was particularly fond of watching wrestlers; however, perhaps to discourage criminal behavior, he made an exception and allowed the blood of condemned prisoners to flow freely. As Rowell explains, over time this only whetted the public appetite for more violent displays:

During a gladiatorial show in . . . the Augustan Age, a notorious Sicilian brigand [named Selurus] was placed on a platform that was contrived to collapse, [dropping] him into a cage of animals that tore him apart. The gruesome theatricality of the event foreshadowed the refinements of cruelty which we meet in the later Empire, when [the] audience demanded and received even stronger fare. So far as our information goes, the Augustan shows were quite humane on the whole in comparison with what followed.[53]

Augustus spent a great deal of money and energy to present one especially note-worthy kind of show, the naumachia. In this staged sea battle, full-sized warships clashed in an artificial lake created especially for the spectacle. The *princeps* must have been unusually proud of these mock fights, for he included this description of one of them in his *Res gestae*:

> I presented to the people an exhibition of a naval battle across the Tiber where the grove of the Caesars now is, having had the site excavated 1,800 feet in length and 1,200 feet in width. In this exhibition thirty beaked ships [that is, equipped with rams on their bows], triremes [with three banks of

A drawing depicts the naumachia, or full-scale naval battle, staged by Augustus, an event he boasted about in his Res gestae.

oars] or biremes [with two banks], and in addition a great number of smaller vessels engaged in combat. On board these fleets, exclusive of rowers, there were about 3,000 combatants.[54]

The Return of Peace and Virtue

Augustus's rebuilding of Rome's infrastructure, introduction of fire and police forces, raising of new temples, theaters, and public forums, and feeding and entertainment of the masses transformed Rome into a great city, one at last befitting its role as leader of the known world. His revitalized capital symbolized the idea of the coming of a new and better age. It appeared to many that the shabby, wartorn, and corrupt Rome of the past was giving way to a more polished, peaceful, and noble Rome.

Augustus strongly emphasized this theme in the Secular Games, a grand religious ceremony he staged in 17 B.C. The dark age of the civil wars was over, the games' message ran, and a new age of peace and prosperity was beginning. The poet Horace, who enjoyed the patronage of the wealthy Maecenas, wrote a hymn, the *Carmen saeculare*, for this special occasion; its words perfectly captured the optimistic mood of the new Augustan Rome: "Already Good Faith and Peace and Honor and the Modesty of olden days and Virtue, so long neglected, muster courage to return, and Plenty with all the riches of its full horn is here for all to see."[55]

Chapter

4 Restoring Roman Family Values: Augustus's Moral Crusade

For Augustus, the ideas of reestablishing social and political order and of championing strict moral values were closely and inevitably linked. When he hailed the return of "faith," "modesty," and "virtue" in the Secular Games in 17 B.C., he established the moral tone of his reign. That tone was conservative, tradition oriented, and in some ways even prudish. His pledge to return Rome to the old-fashioned "family values" of the past was motivated partly by the belief then generally accepted by a majority of Romans, namely that those cherished values had been lost. According to this view, the chaos and corruption of the late republican era was caused, to a great extent, by moral decay, which had infected both government leaders and the people themselves.

On the most fundamental level, people believed, there had been a breakdown in the strict religious rituals and practices that had guided the early Romans in their rise to world power status. The traditional Roman view was that religious ritual was absolutely necessary to maintain a well-ordered society, of which the basic unit was not the individual, but the family. The main purpose of the rituals of sacrifice and prayer were to appease the gods and thereby to secure the continued well-

being of the family group and, by extension, society in general. Supposedly, by neglecting such rituals and following their own selfish desires, state leaders and others had disrupted Rome's sacred relationship with the gods and the divine punishment had been decades of civil strife, death, and misery. Thus, as Donald Earl points out, "when Augustus repaired temples, restored cults, and encouraged the state religion, this formed an essential and inescapable part of his reestablishment of a stable and ordered society."[56]

Undoubtedly, Augustus's moral crusade was also personally motivated. He was an avowed family man who took great interest and pride in the accomplishments of his wife, children, and other relatives. So the apparent breakdown of the Roman family distressed him. He was also deeply religious and more superstitious about omens and divine wrath than the average person of his time. According to Suetonius:

As for Augustus's attitude toward religion: he is recorded to have been scared of thunder and lightning [which he believed were signs the gods were angry], against which he always carried a piece of seal-skin as an amulet, and to have taken refuge in an

Augustus and various members of his family are depicted in formal dress and noble procession in this panel from the Ara Pacis Augustae, *or Altar of Augustan Peace, erected by the* princeps *in the Campus Martius in 13* B.C.

underground vault whenever a heavy storm threatened.[57]

Thus it is hardly surprising that the *princeps* often displayed puritanical, or very strict and old-fashioned, attitudes in both his personal and public life and that he so strongly encouraged the return of moral values.

Patching Up the Divine Contract

The religious beliefs and values that Augustus and many others sought to restore were deeply rooted in Rome's past. Ancient Roman religion comprised a complex and very formal set of rites and practices designed to maintain a good working relationship between the gods and humans. The earliest Romans wor-

shiped spirits they thought resided in everything around them, including inanimate objects like rocks and trees. This kind of belief system is known as animism. The early household spirits were called the numina, who were divided into the penates, who protected the family food storage; the lares, who kept the home safe and also guarded streets and crossroads; and the manes, spirits of deceased ancestors, who watched over various family members.

At first, the Romans pictured these spirits as natural forces rather than as formal deities. In time, however, some spirits began to take on humanlike personalities. These became gods and goddesses, such as Vesta, the goddess of the hearth; Janus, who watched over the doorway; and Mars, who protected farmers' fields. Over the centuries, the Romans, a highly adaptive people who borrowed much from other cultures, incorporated foreign religious concepts and gods, particularly those of the Etruscans and Greeks, into their own faith. Thus, the Etruscan sky god, Jupiter, and the Greek head god, Zeus, merged into the Roman head god, Jupiter. And the Roman field protector, Mars, became associated with and eventually assumed the same identity as Ares, the Greek god of war. Meanwhile, many of the early household spirits, including the lares, were maintained and worshiped right alongside the more powerful deities.

The relationship that developed between these gods and the Romans who worshiped them was in the form of a sacred contract. As Henry Rowell states:

> The Roman attitude toward his gods has been summarized in the formula *do ut des*—"I give [to you the god] so that you may give [to me the mortal]." This emphasizes the legalistic and contractual aspect of Roman religion.[58]

Early Romans make a sacrifice to Jupiter, the head god, also called Invictus, *The Invincible, and* Divis pater, *Father of Heaven.*

Thus, mortals agreed to respect, pay homage to, and sacrifice to the gods and in return the gods agreed to grant mortals a certain degree of order and prosperity.

Since the general belief in the early days of Augustus's reign was that this divine contract had been broken by the preceding several generations of Romans, he saw it both as his duty and as a political necessity to patch up the agreement. He attempted to bolster the old faith in a number of ways. First, in 28 B.C., even before he received his new name of Augustus, he undertook the swift, wholesale renovation of more than eighty temples that had fallen into disrepair. And he paid for these projects mostly from his own pockets. This demonstrated to the people that he was genuinely concerned about Rome's religious life.

Augustus also took on the responsibilities of the office of *pontifex maximus,* the religious head of state and in a sense the pope of the Roman religion. These duties included leading the rituals during major religious festivals and making all the major decisions involving Rome's temples, shrines, and religious holidays. At first, however, he could not assume the title itself. This was because his old triumviral partner Lepidus had been proclaimed the official pontiff several years before and had the right to remain so until his death. So Augustus actually ran the office until Lepidus finally died in 12 B.C., at which time the *princeps* became pontiff in name as well as fact. As such, he symbolized the union of state and religion, the only human-made partnership that seemed strong enough to bring lasting order to the empire.

As *pontifex maximus,* Augustus steadily restored the dignity of the Roman faith.

This statue of Augustus as a priest of the state religion shows him with his head covered to emphasize his piety.

He increased the number of priests, men specially trained to lead public religious ceremonies and to recognize and interpret omens. And he revived, in a lavish and solemn manner, several sacred ceremonies and festivals, including the Secular Games, that had been neglected for many years. In addition, John Firth writes, Augustus

restored the worship of the lares, the minor deities of the street and the home [whom many Romans of the late republic had come to ignore], by raising three hundred little shrines at the crossways and street corners of the city, and by ordering that twice a year, in spring and summer, their modest altars should be adorned with flowers. Due honor to the gods, both great and small, was the cardinal principle of Augustus in dealing with religion.[59]

The Roman Family

Religious revivals were only part of Augustus's agenda for restoring conservative Roman values. He also sought to influence and even to legislate social attitudes, customs, and practices. Before the Augustan Age, such customs as marriage, divorce, and child rearing were strictly private affairs. The Roman family was a tightly knit unit presided over by the paterfamilias, the eldest adult male, usually both husband and father, who had the final word in family decisions. His wife or mother was the materfamilias, who kept the household running smoothly and looked after the children.

Unlike Greek women, who led sheltered lives and spent most of their time shut up in the "women's quarters," Roman women were considered nearly equal to men and actively participated in household decision making and various social events.[60] By tradition, husbands, wives, fathers, and mothers all had a sacred duty to uphold and perpetuate a strong, loyal family unit. Thus, such activities as adultery,

Members of an upper-class Roman family confer near the entrance to their peristyle, or walled garden. In the early republic, the paterfamilias, seen at right, exercised absolute power over his wife and children.

divorce, or betrayal of a relative were severely frowned upon.

But during the last century or so of the republic, many (although certainly not all) Romans became lax about their marital and parental duties and family ties began to weaken. Rowell comments:

> The old standards of marital morality began to fall in the second century B.C. before the wealth which came to the city from the conquests in the East [mainly the Greek-ruled kingdoms]. With the wealth came greed, a taste for luxuries . . . and new, more "sophisticated" ways of acting and thinking. . . . The ruthless pursuit of wealth and power and the placing of personal ambition before the common good naturally determined standards of conduct in private relations.[61]

Under these conditions, adultery became more common and so did divorce, which was often used as a convenient tool with which to dump one's spouse and marry one's lover. As in all ages, children suffered most from such broken marriages.

And in general, as people increasingly engaged in sex more for fun than for having children, the birthrate declined.

Legislating Morality

Augustus sought to restore the respect and dignity of the marriage institution and the integrity of the family, the rock on which the Roman state had been built. He also wanted to increase the birthrate. In ancient times, when the success and survival of a nation was often determined by the sheer size of its army and the civilian ranks supplying it, a declining population was seen as dangerous and undesirable.

As a first step, in 18 B.C. the government, under Augustus's direction, tried to discourage adultery by issuing a law making it a crime. Under this statute, the *lex Julia de adulteriis coercendis*, if a man and woman were caught having an affair outside of marriage they could be dragged into public court and if convicted suffer serious punishment. This consisted of having to live on separate islands for the rest of their lives, losing the right to remarry, and forfeiting much of their personal property.

Between 18 B.C. and A.D. 9, the *princeps* also pushed through laws, among them the *lex Julia de maritandis ordinibus*, designed to promote marriage and child bearing. Essentially, the statutes offered rewards, such as political privileges or tax relief, to couples who stayed together and had lots of children. They also carried penalties for those who did not. Unmarried adults or childless married couples lost the right to inherit money and property (except when the deceased relative was a soldier) and unmarried and childless women who owned property had to pay a special tax on that property.

In addition, Augustus issued numerous individual prudish and puritanical

Tragedy in the Imperial Family

Augustus was anything but a hypocrite. He applied the same strict moral code he had imposed on his subjects to himself and his own family and did not hesitate to prosecute and punish his only child, Julia, for committing what he deemed one of the worst possible offenses—adultery. In this excerpt from his compelling biography Augustus, *John Buchan describes this tragic incident, which occurred in 2 B.C.*

"Julia in Rome lived wholly among the younger set, and stories began to circulate of her doings. She was seen with drunken revelers in the streets, and was a frequent guest at dubious male parties. Tiberius [her husband and Augustus's stepson by Livia] was well aware of the scandals and suffered them in silence. . . . Then suddenly Augustus learned from Livia what was happening, since all Rome rang with the story. He was wounded to the quick in his pride and self-respect. At the very time when he was attempting to purify Roman morals his own child was revealed [to have committed adultery, an act] which he detested. . . . He referred the business to the [law court of the] Senate and asked for the legal penalty. Her two chief lovers were a son of Mark Antony . . . and the younger Gracchus [Sempronius, descendant of two renowned patriots and social reformers]; the former committed suicide [as his father had after Actium] and the latter was banished. Julia herself was exiled to the island of Pandataria, off the Campanian coast [northwest of modern Naples]. Such was the fate of this bright . . . creature who, under happier circumstances, might have been great, for she had an excellent mind. . . . Neither her father nor her husband ever saw her again . . . and, though she was later allowed to live on the [Italian] mainland, her exile was never rescinded."

A sheep is prepared for sacrifice during a Roman wedding ceremony.

edits that attempted to legislate against "lewd" or "immoral" public displays, especially those that might "corrupt" young children. Firth cites the following examples:

> He forbade boys from taking part in the *Lupercalia* [fertility rites featuring footraces in which males dressed in blood-smeared goatskins]; at the Secular Games he issued an edict that no young person should attend the evening performances [consisting of lavish banquets and the bloody sacrifices of various animals] unless in the company of an elder relative. At the gladiatorial shows he restricted women to the upper parts of the amphitheater [to keep them from seeing cuts and bruises up close]; to athletic festivals [in which men competed wearing very little] he denied [women] entrance altogether.[62]

He also imposed strict discipline on theater audiences and actors. Spectators, usually loud and rowdy, had to restrain themselves, and actors, most of whom

were considered social outcasts, were warned not to do anything to offend traditional family values. Suetonius described one celebrated incident:

> When [Augustus] heard that Stephanio, a Roman actor, went about attended by a page-boy who was really a married woman with her hair cropped [short], he had him flogged through all the three theaters—those of Pompey, Balbus, and Marcellus—and then exiled him.[63]

A Simple, Frugal Man

Suetonius and other ancient writers told about the enactment of such laws and edicts but were more vague about whether they achieved the desired effect and improved public morality. It is more probable that, like similar attempts to legislate morality in other ages, these laws mainly made people more careful not to get caught. But the fact that many of the social statutes Augustus passed remained on the books for centuries reveals an important facet of the Roman character. Apparently, the traditionally conservative Romans welcomed setting limits on their behavior, even if most people occasionally exceeded those limits. This demonstrates that Augustus was closely in touch with his people's character and temperament.

But what of his own character? Did Augustus follow the moral guidelines he set for others and therefore deserve the respect and love the people lavished on him? It would seem that he did. In addition to being very religious and family oriented, Augustus lived a simple, frugal life that greatly contrasted with his enormously powerful and prestigious position. His wife, Livia, sister Octavia, and daughter Julia made almost all of his clothes, which were mostly plain. His house on the summit of the Palatine Hill, made of plain stone rather than marble, had but twelve rooms, only five of which he and Livia normally used. They lived there for more than forty years, projecting the image of the traditional Roman couple, content with simple pleasures and dutiful family life, despite the fact that they were the wealthiest couple in the known world.

Augustus's simplicity and frugality extended to his eating and drinking habits. His favorite meal consisted of a piece of coarse bread, a few sardines, and a slab of cheese, the usual dinner fare of Roman laborers. Since he considered drunkenness unseemly and immoral, he was also careful to restrict his wine intake. According to Suetonius:

> Augustus was a habitually abstemious [moderate] drinker. . . . He never took more than three drinks of wine-and-water at dinner. In later life his limit was a pint; if he ever exceeded this he would deliberately vomit. . . . He seldom touched wine between meals; instead, he would moisten his throat with a morsel of bread dunked in cold water; or a slice of cucumber or the heart of a young lettuce.[64]

In keeping with his public image, that of the traditional upstanding, diligent, and strict-but-just Roman paterfamilias, Augustus proved to be a hardworking and fair leader. The long hours he spent judging court cases and the just sentences he handed down constitute a clear example. Under his new order, the Senate often acted as a kind of supreme court that heard cases involving crimes against the state, and as head of that state he reserved the right to be final judge in cases that interested or particularly disturbed him. According to Suetonius's account, he often stayed in the Senate House hearing cases well into the night. And when ill, he convened court in his home at his bedside, apparently not in the least uneasy about having people see him so enfeebled. His fairness was illustrated by his acquittal of witnesses to a forged will. The law stated that such persons had to be found guilty even when they had no idea that the document they had signed was a phony. But the *princeps* insisted on allowing for deception and human error.

An idealized portrait of Augustus and his wife, Livia, who was known for her intelligence and generosity.

Quite a Humble Dwelling

Here, from his book Augustus and Nero, *scholar Gilbert Charles-Picard describes Augustus's modest house on the Palatine Hill, which was excavated in 1869 and is referred to by modern Italians as the Casa di Livia.*

"In 44 B.C. Octavian . . . bought a villa on the Palatine which had belonged to the orator Hortensius, a rival to Cicero. In spite of the owner's celebrity, it was quite a humble dwelling, without mosaics [expensive tiles] or marbles. . . . The house consists of a main apartment of five rooms, with additional rooms making a total of twelve. Its plan follows that of the traditional Roman house, centered on the *atrium*, the common- or living-room, which originally contained the hearth and had an opening in the middle of the roof for the smoke to escape and for rain-water to be collected. Visitors today enter the house through the *atrium*, now completely uncovered, and see ahead three rectangular rooms opening from it; they are the *tablinum*, the master's study, and its 'wings.' On the right is another rectangular room, which is no doubt the *triclinium*, the dining-room. All these are now several feet below ground level [although in Augustus's time they rested on the hill's surface]."

The Spread of the Imperial Cult

Augustus maintained his image as a simple, moral man of the people in another way. Despite his lofty position and sweeping powers, he was careful neither to act in a superior manner nor to accept undue flattery. Suetonius recorded that

> He always felt horrified and insulted when called "My Lord." Once, while he was watching a comedy [in a theater], one of the players spoke the line: "O just and generous Lord!" whereupon the entire audience rose to their feet and applauded, as if the phrase referred to Augustus. A look and a gesture soon quelled this unsuitable flattery, and the next day he issued an edict of stern reprimand [ordering that no one should call him that].[65]

Yet interestingly, Augustus seemed to apply and enforce this edict only in Rome and the heartland of the empire. By contrast, in Egypt he was seen as the natural successor to the semidivine Egyptian pharaohs and worshiped literally as a god. And in Greece and many other parts to the east, people hailed him as their savior and benefactor and prayed and sacrificed to his image. Some of these groups went further and began worshiping the Augustan dynasty, Augustus's family line, from which would come his successors. Thus began the phenomenon of the "imperial cult," the worship of the Roman chief of state as a living god.

Augustus not only tolerated such cults, but for political reasons actually encouraged them. "While excessive adulation [praise] might arouse suspicion in Rome," Earl points out, "Augustus's acceptance of divine honors was an act of policy to bind the peoples of the East more closely to him . . . as the head and embodiment of the Roman state."[66] Thus, just as he had with republican traditions in Rome, in the eastern lands Augustus shrewdly exploited existing customs and traditions to consolidate and maintain his own authority. In a sense, the imperial cult became part of his overall promotion of ancient tradition, especially religious tradition, to maintain order all over the empire.

It was perhaps inevitable that the concept of the imperial cult would eventually spread to Rome, even though the Romans themselves had no native tradition of a divine ruler. The initial Roman worship of Augustus began in a relatively subtle way when he was proclaimed *pontifex maximus* in 12 B.C. Traditionally, a new pontiff moved to a residence set aside especially for him in the main Forum, but Augustus preferred to stay in his modest house on the Palatine. According to custom, the pontiff's home was public and sacred ground and the spirits that attended that home were revered in the state religion by all Romans. So from that time on, people began worshiping the lares of Augustus's family home.

They also worshiped his genius, or guardian spirit. The Romans believed each family had its own special guardian that inhabited the master of the house, the paterfamilias, and secured the continuity of the family line by passing from father to son. In a very real sense, Augustus's genius now ensured the continuity of the entire Roman people, who, because he was both political and religious head of state, constituted his larger family.

The worship of Augustus's lares and genius spread quickly throughout Italy and then to western provinces such as Spain and Gaul. Earl explains:

> In Italy in addition to the crossroads shrines to the *Lares* and the *Genius* [of Augustus] there arose special temples for the *Genius*, called *Augustea*, which had their own priests. The cult, in other words, became . . . a municipal concern, in which all members of the community . . . participated. The importance of the municipal cult was increased by the creation of new offices, half-priestly and half-administrative, called *Augustales*.[67]

Another Way to Maintain Order

Augustus approved of the form the imperial cult took in Italy and the western part of the empire and encouraged its spread. If this cult had been more overt and worshiped him openly as a living god, as many eastern cults did, he would have rejected it outright. He had gone to great pains, after all, to avoid the titles and trappings of a king and the Roman people would surely frown on his pretending to be divine.

However, his household spirits, and not Augustus himself, were the focus of

Trying Hard to Get to Sleep

The princeps *was such a dedicated and hardworking leader that he adjusted his sleeping schedule around his duties, as documented by this excerpt from* Suetonius's Lives of the Twelve Caesars. *This account is based on the testimony of Augustus's associates, scribes, and servants.*

"When dinner was over he would retire to a couch in his study, where he worked late until all the outstanding business of the day had been cleared off; or most of it. Then he went to bed and slept seven hours at the outside, with three or four breaks of wakefulness. If he found it hard to fall asleep again . . . as frequently happened, he sent for readers or story-tellers [to help make him drowsy]. . . . He could not bear lying sleepless in the dark with no one by his side; and if he had to officiate at some official or religious ceremony that involved early rising—which he also loathed—would spend the previous night at a friend's house as near the appointed place as possible. Even so, he often needed more sleep than he got, and would doze off during his journeys through the city on his litter [couch carried by servants]."

worship in the west. By modern standards the difference between the two seems trivial, particularly since his genius was thought to dwell within his body, but to the Romans the distinction between the man and his spirits was clear-cut and significant. More importantly, the people viewed public worship of his personal numina as a natural and perfectly legal extension of religious custom. Thus, Augustus had shrewdly found still another way to use accepted tradition to bolster his own image and to maintain order and control.

Augustus's endeavors in the areas of religion and morality had long-term effects even he could not have foreseen. His attempts to control people's moral attitudes and his manipulation of the imperial cult phenomenon set in motion important changes in the way Romans saw their rulers. Later emperors would build on his precedents to create the very thing he tried to avoid: a kingly and divine status for the Roman chief of state. The man who hated to be called lord unwittingly spawned a long line of lordly successors.

Chapter

5 Triumph of the Spirit: The Golden Age of Roman Literature

Like most Romans who lived in the era immediately following the end of the civil wars, popular writers were optimistic and enthusiastic about the more peaceful, more constructive, and seemingly more civilized world Augustus was bringing about. All around them society was changing, leaving behind the fear and chaos of the past and embracing a brave new future. It was only natural, then, that various aspects of the new political and moral order figured as prominent themes in their works.

Augustus himself, with his keen sense of the power of propaganda, realized that the written word was a powerful tool he could use to promote his various programs and his emphasis on Rome's mission to bring order to the whole world. This motive, coupled with his genuine love of literature and ideas, led him to encourage thinkers and writers. "Augustus gave all possible encouragement to intellectuals," Suetonius wrote. "He would politely and patiently attend readings not only of their poems and historical works, but of their speeches and dialogues."[68]

However, writers in Augustan Rome received much more than sincere moral and verbal support. At Augustus's urging, many of his wealthy friends patronized, or provided complete financial support for,

writers and artists, allowing them to create at their leisure without having to worry about making a living. Augustus's close associate Maecenas became the greatest literary patron of the age. Most of its best-known and beloved writers, including Virgil, Horace, and Propertius, became part of Maecenas's elite literary circle.

An upper-class Roman sits reading scrolls in his sumptuously decorated library.

The result of so many talented individuals' receiving such generous support from society's highest levels was a literary outpouring greater in scope and quality than Rome had ever produced or would ever again produce. The Augustan Age of literature, usually dated from the death of the republican writer-orator Cicero in 43 B.C. to the death of the Augustan poet Ovid in A.D. 17, eventually came to be seen as Rome's literary golden age. The works of the Augustan writers had a profound and lasting impact, not only on later Roman society, but also on the literature and philosophy of later medieval and modern Europe.

Laboring over Every Word and Phrase

The qualities that made Augustan literature unique and important become apparent after examining the nature of earlier Roman literature. The early Romans were not a particularly artistic or inventive people, as were the more cultured Greeks, and as a result Latin literature got off to a slow start. Not until the third century B.C., after their conquest of the Italian Greek cities had brought them into contact with Greek culture, did the Romans begin producing their own native writings. And for a long time these works were simply Latin versions of Greek subjects and literary forms.

For instance, the third-century-B.C. Roman writers Gnaeus Naevius and Quintus Ennius wrote epic poems, book-length sets of verses describing wars and other heroic events. These works strictly followed the form and the meter, the rhythmic pattern of the words and lines, of the *Iliad* and the *Odyssey*, the epics about the Trojan War and its aftermath that were attributed to the legendary Greek poet Homer. And the second-century-B.C. Roman playwrights Plautus and Terence openly copied the characters, themes, and even the plots of plays by Menander and other renowned Greek writers.

Indeed, as scholar Garry Wills points out, "The great continuing challenge to Roman identity came from Greece. The Romans seemed to have sensed from the outset that their fate depended on the terms of their accommodation to [absorption of and submission to] Greek thought."[69] Even Cicero, who strongly maintained that Roman character and government were superior to those of the Greeks, was steeped in Greek philosophy and regularly supported his arguments with references to Greek thinkers such as Plato and Aristotle. Augustan writers, following closely on the heels of Cicero and other republican writers, were also heavily influenced by Greek ideas and literary forms. After all, perhaps the greatest work of the period, Virgil's *Aeneid*, was an epic poem in the Homeric style. Even its subject—the fall of Troy—was the same.

But Augustan literature was characterized by qualities earlier Roman writings lacked. First, the Augustan writers ably captured the sincere feelings of relief, joy, optimism, and renewal that permeated their times, making their works extremely vigorous and passionate. These writers also labored diligently over every word, phrase, and line, striving, like none before them, to achieve the most perfect and beautiful forms possible. In doing so, they took full advantage of the exceptional qualities of the Latin language, which was very different than Greek. In fact, Michael Grant states, Latin gave these works considerable originality because it "proved able to create both resonant [full and pleasing], vigorously compact prose and poetry of stirringly profound, harmonious musicality."[70] Many of the finest of Europe's later writers greatly admired and tried to imitate the preciseness and overall beauty of Augustan literature.

In addition, many of the Augustan writers took full advantage of one literary form that was uniquely Roman. This was the love elegy, a series of verses, sometimes written over several years, in which a poet described his changing relationship with a woman, usually his mistress. Roman readers became intimately familiar with the joys and frustrations Ovid experienced with Corinna, Propertius with Cynthia, and Tibullus with Delia.[71] Not surprisingly, love, with its many pleasures and disap-

pointments, became one of the principal literary themes of the new age.

Other important themes writers employed, of course, were those that glorified Augustus's special brand of Roman nationalism. These included peace, which promised to last forever; the imperial mission of Rome and Italy to rule the world; the beauties of Italy and its fields and farms; praise of Augustus, his family, and his spirits; the revival of religion and traditional Roman virtues and morals; and the glories of Rome's heroic pre–civil war past. Many centuries later, Europeans would marvel at and envy the idealized image of a mighty, noble, and heroic Rome that Augustan writers created.

Moral Earnestness and Burning Patriotism

One Augustan writer managed to capture this idealized vision of Rome so consistently and in such a grand manner that he became the most popular and influential literary figure of the age. He was Publius Vergilius Maro, commonly known as Virgil. Born in 70 B.C., he grew up on a farm in northern Italy and, like most rural Romans, came to love the land and the virtues of agricultural life, which later became major themes in his works. Shortly after the Battle of Philippi in 42 B.C., Virgil met Maecenas and, through him, the young Octavian. The poet soon made his name with the *Eclogues*, a collection of short poems about country life, and then worked for seven years on another set of pastoral verses, the *Georgics*, finished just in time for Octavian's triumphant return to Rome in 29 B.C. Thereafter, until his

The poet Virgil, Rome's most revered writer, is flanked by two of the Muses, the legendary daughters of the god Zeus, each of whom presided over a specific branch of the arts.

death ten years later, Virgil was the most respected and imitated writer in the known world.

Virgil had many literary talents but his greatest was his ability to capture a vision of and make people feel genuine nostalgia for the "good old days." As John Firth puts it:

> The great secret of the power which he wielded over his contemporaries and over the ages which were to follow lies not so much in . . . his moral earnestness and in the spirit of humanity . . . which permeates his work. . . . Deep religion and intense burning patriotism—in these lie the secret of Virgil's influence. . . . He looked back with regret to the bygone days when men lived simpler lives, and not only feared, but walked with, the gods.[72]

Virgil's talent for dramatizing the heroic characters and events of past ages reached its zenith in his masterpiece, the epic poem the *Aeneid*. In this definitive version of the old Roman legend, after escaping the burning Troy and traveling around the Mediterranean in search of a new home Aeneas eventually reaches the western shore of Italy. There he meets a local prophetess named Sibyl, who guides him into the underworld to see his dead father, Anchises. The old man's spirit reveals to Aeneas a vision of the future that includes his descendant Romulus founding Rome, the Romans' rise to greatness, and finally the coming of Augustus, whose Rome will encompass the known world. Anchises declares:

> Here is the very man whom you have heard so often promised you [in prophecy], Augustus Caesar, your child of the Divine who shall refound a golden age for Latium—in those lands, those very lands where Saturn once was king, who shall extend the frontier of our rule [to the edges of the world, lands that lie] outside the track of stars, outside the course of the year and of the sun, where Atlas the sky-bearer humps on his shoulder the spinning pole of the world.[73]

Inspired by this vision, Aeneas sails up the Tiber and fights battles with Latium's early inhabitants. Eventually, peace is achieved and he marries a Latin bride, planting the seed for the coming master race.

It is not difficult to understand why this plot and these themes so appealed to the Romans of Virgil's day. He put into stirring prose and verse the Romans' deep pride in their past and their belief that they had a superior destiny. Summing up Virgil's appeal to his countrymen, historian R. H. Barrow writes:

> The most significant movement of history . . . according to Virgil, is the march of the Roman along the road of his destiny to a high civilization; for in that destiny is to be found the valid and permanent interpretation of all [human] movement and all development. . . . The stately *Aeneid* progresses throughout its length to this theme, the universal and the ultimate triumph of the Roman spirit as the highest manifestation of man's powers.[74]

The Easygoing Horace, the Daring Ovid

Another important writer in Maecenas's literary circle, one who attained nearly as large a reputation as Virgil, was Quintus Horatius Flaccus, popularly known as Horace. Born the son of a former slave in 65 B.C., Horace studied in the best schools in Athens and Rome and then entered the republican army raised in Greece by Brutus and Cassius. At the Battle of Philippi, the poet, who later admitted that he was not cut out to be a soldier, was so afraid that he fled the field in terror. Soon afterward he went to Rome and there had the good fortune to meet Virgil, who recognized his talents and introduced him to Maecenas and Octavian. About 37 B.C., Horace achieved financial independence and all the leisure time he needed for writing when Maecenas provided him with a country estate staffed by an overseer, five tenant farmers, and eight slaves.

While both Virgil and Horace strove for the same level of polished language and perfect form, their personalities and styles were very different. Donald Dudley points out that "Virgil was introspective [wrapped up in his own thoughts] and melancholy, brooding on distant and receding horizons [visions of long ago]. Horace lived on the surface of life and for the pleasures of the moment."[75] In contrast to the lofty, heroic, and generally serious tone of Virgil's works, Horace's poetry explored and commented on everyday situations, feelings, and emotions, usually in an easygoing or humorous way.

Horace's general view of life was that it was short and uncertain, that death was inevitable, and that a person could only achieve immortality by creating or achieving something of lasting value. Therefore, it made sense to enjoy life and its pleasures, including love and wine, although not to gross and unseemly excess. Ho-

This painting of the poet Horace captures his urbane, easygoing, and pleasant manner.

race's philosophy of living and enjoying one day at a time is evident in this excerpt from one of his *Odes*:

Happy the man, and happy he alone,
  he who can call today his own;
He who, secure within, can say:

"Tomorrow do your worst, for I have lived today.

Be fair, or foul, or rain, or shine, the joys I have possessed, in spite of fate, are mine.

Not heaven itself upon the past has power; but what has been, has been, and I have had my hour."[76]

Although Horace's poetry extolled life's pleasures, including love and sex, it was rarely sexually explicit. In contrast, many of the love poems of Publius Ovidius Naso, known as Ovid, were quite daring and explicit, and while many Romans enjoyed them, many others were shocked and offended. Born in 43 B.C., Ovid was much younger than his celebrated contemporaries Virgil and Horace and was never invited into Maecenas's circle. Ovid's mentor was another wealthy arts patron named Corvinus Messala.

Ovid utilized a number of different poetic forms, including the love letter, but most of all he was a master of the love elegy. His love poems were generally witty and full of delicate, colorful description. Despite their beauty, however, many discussed private sexual matters in a manner too open and graphic for more conservative Romans like Augustus, and this inevitably got the poet into trouble. Literary scholar Bernard Knox suggests that the *princeps* was "scandalized" by Ovid's first book of poems, the *Amores*, which were

a witty, audacious chronicle of the author's love life with a married woman [Corinna]. . . . Ovid followed this up with the *Ars amatoria* [*Erotic Technique*], a handbook of seduction, part one addressed to men, part two to women. The closing lines of the second part

---

We Will Tread the Gloomy Way Together

In this excerpt from an ode dedicated to Maecenas, quoted in Latin Literature in Translation, *Horace extolled his patron's virtues and suggested that if Maecenas died, his humble follower Horace would rather die too than live without him.*

No! My Maecenas, no! the gods and I
Are clearly averse [against the idea] that you should die;
My best support, my patron, or to blend
Every dear name in one, my honored friend,
Cease these complaints, it cannot, must not be,
That you should see Elysium [heaven] without me. . . .
Have I not sworn, nor will I break my oath,
The call of death for one will summon both;
When, or however you may the journey make,
I am resolved its perils to partake;
We will together, tread the gloomy way,
Together, seek the realms of brighter day.

Ovid (43 B.C.–A.D. 17) wrote highly passionate and descriptive poetry that gained a wide and devoted audience, but his style was often too explicit for the prudish Augustus.

give explicit advice to the fair sex on the positions for sexual intercourse best suited for their figures and complexions.[77]

Following are a few of the least explicit lines from the *Ars amatoria*'s advice to men: "After a woman passes [the age of] thirty-five, her gifts are ripe, for Nature has endowed her with [lovemaking] skills unknown to girls of seventeen. Let the impatient [man] drink the new-made wine; I'll take deep swallows from rich and well-stocked cellars."[78]

The prudish Augustus was indeed scandalized by what he saw as Ovid's loose morals. However, perhaps because he wanted to avoid the image of an uncultured dictator who suppressed intellectuals, the *princeps* tolerated Ovid's audacity for many years. But eventually the ax fell.

For reasons that remain unclear (some rumors claimed the poet was somehow involved with Augustus's daughter Julia), in A.D. 8 Ovid was exiled to Tomi, a bleak frontier town on the shores of the Black Sea. He died there nine years later.

The Colossal Ruins of Livy's History

Augustan literature was not confined to poetry. The outstanding prose writer of the age, and the most popular of all Roman historians, not only in his own day, but ever since, was Titus Livius, known as Livy. Born in 59 B.C. in Patavium (now Padua) in northern Italy, Livy spent most of his life in Rome, where he witnessed firsthand the fall of the republic and rise of the *Principate*. At Augustus's urging, he devoted much of his life to a massive and detailed history of Rome, *From the Founding of the City*, which covered events from Aeneas's legendary arrival in Italy to about 9 B.C. Of the original 142 volumes, only 35 have survived.

Measured by any standard, ancient or modern, Livy's achievement was monumental. J. Wight Duff states:

> No Augustan prose writer is for a moment comparable with Livy. His prose-epic is . . . sister to the *Aeneid*. Not even in Virgil has the greatness of the Roman character found a more dignified or more lasting monument than in the colossal ruins of Livy's history.[79]

Evaluated in a modern light, Livy did not always use the best sources of information and his facts were not always accurate. Also, his narrative was riddled with references to

Livy (59 B.C.–A.D. 17), whose masterwork, Ab urbe condita, *or* From the Founding of the City, *covered the entire history of Rome from the days of the legendary Aeneas to 9 B.C.*

such an approach to history would be considered biased and patronizing. But in Livy's day it was seen as natural and very praiseworthy, and so Livy personified the spirit of Augustus's moral crusade. Scholar Kevin Guinagh comments in *Latin Literature in Translation*:

> Livy's purpose in writing his history was definitely moral. To his practical Roman mind there was little value in simply recording facts accurately for the sake of facts. He was always at pains to teach a lesson so that the corrupt citizens of his decadent [sinful] age might be won [over] to . . . the stoic virtues that characterized their ancestors.[80]

Livy summed up this approach himself, writing: "In history, fortunately, you can find a record of the ample range of human experience clearly set up for everyone to see; in that record, you may discover for yourself and for your country, examples and warning."[81]

No doubt Livy's success also stemmed from the fact that his narrative read more like an adventure story than a straightforward scholarly work. Even though he omitted or colored some of the facts, he ably captured the romantic spirit and majestic sweep of Rome's long history and thereby made that history accessible and appealing to the average person. The following excerpt, describing the prelude to the Battle of Magnesium in 190 B.C. between the Romans and Seleucid Greeks, illustrates his use of detail to add color and to build suspense:

> A morning mist, lightening into clouds as the day advanced, caused a fog; the moisture from this, like a rain

omens and fate directing the course of historical events, although he himself tended to be skeptical about such supernatural forces.

What, then, made Livy's writing great? Part of the answer was his genius for capturing the colorful personalities of the great leaders and other historical figures he cited. Also, Livy's chosen style was to praise, condemn, or otherwise criticize the characters and events he chronicled in order to teach his readers a lesson. Today, brought on by the west wind, covered everything; these conditions brought absolutely no discomfort to the Romans, but . . . they were very inconvenient for the [Seleucid] king's army; for the faintness of the light . . . did not deprive the Romans of a view in all directions, and the moisture . . . did not at all dull their swords and spears; [but] the king's troops . . . could not see the flanks [far sides of the battle formation] even from the center . . . and the moisture had softened their bowstrings and slings and the thongs of their javelins.[82]

A Gift to Posterity

Livy's great work became such an instant classic that no other writers of his time tried to compete with him in the field of history. So, like Virgil, Horace, and Ovid, other Augustan writers stuck to poetry. Of the three best-known, Sextus Propertius and Lucius Varius Rufus, known simply as Varius, were friends of Virgil's and members of Maecenas's prestigious literary group, and Albius Tibullus, like Ovid, enjoyed the patronage of Messala. Varius wrote mainly epic poems; both Virgil and

The Blessings of Peace

Albius Tibullus (ca. 54–19 B.C.) was an avowed pacifist, which made him a rarity among Roman men. The elegies he produced in his short career were filled with references to peace, love, and pastoral simplicity, as in this excerpt (quoted from Guinagh and Dorjahn's Latin Literature in Translation*) from one listing the many blessings of peace.*

Who was the man who first forged the fatal blade?
  Oh! cruel he [was] and of an iron soul!
Then war and carnage first made gory raid,
  Opening a shorter way to life's dreary goal [death]. . . .

Peace dwell with us! fair Peace and nothing else before
  Yoked the curved plow to the sturdy steer [ox];
Peace reared the vine [and] with vine-juice filled the store [storage bins]
  With which the sire [father] his loving son might cheer. . . .

Let savage warriors wield the sword and spear,
  But keep aloof [away] from the gentle damsel's door;
Come bounteous Peace! still hold the wheaten ear [crops],
  And from your joyous lap rich fruits outpour.

"Quicker than Boiled Asparagus"

It is unfortunate that Augustus's own informal writings are lost, for they supposedly contained a number of unique and quaint words and phrases, as Suetonius recorded in Lives of the Twelve Caesars.

"Augustus's everyday language must have contained many whimsical expressions of his own coinage [invention], to judge from letters in his own handwriting [many of which still existed in Suetonius's time]. . . . [His] favorite metaphor for swift and sudden actions: 'Quicker than boiled asparagus.' Here is a list of unusual synonyms which constantly appear in Augustus's letters:

baceolus (dolt) for: *stultus* (fool); *pulleiaceus* (woodenheaded) for: *cerritus* (crazy); *vapide se habere* (feel flat) for: *male se habere* (feel bad); *betizare* (be a beetroot) for: *languere* (be languid). . . .

Among his grammatical peculiarities . . . I have noticed one particular habit. . . . Rather than break a long word at the end of a line and carry forward to the next whatever letters were left over, he would write these underneath the first part of the word and draw a loop to connect them with it."

Horace admired and sometimes copied his style and ideas. When Virgil died, leaving his majestic *Aeneid* unfinished, Varius completed and edited the work. Propertius and Tibullus were, along with Ovid, the masters of the love elegy and of love poems in general.

From a literary standpoint, Propertius was perhaps the most important of the three. His writing had a particularly passionate, sensitive, and sincere tone that influenced the style of Italian writers during and after the European Renaissance, more than twelve centuries after his death. He was also preoccupied with death: how it snatched people away from the beauties of life and also how true love could tran-

scend it. Propertius expressed these themes in this elegant and moving excerpt from one of his *Elegies*, in which a dead wife addresses the husband she left behind:

Paullus, I leave you as a pledge of my
  love our children:
Guard them; this care still burns in my
  dead heart.
Their hands seek yours; their arms lie
  round your shoulders.
You must take a father's and now a
  mother's part. . . .
Long haunted nights—how many of
  them wait you,
With dreams [in which she appears]
  to break the heart and trick the eye.

O when you speak in secret to my phantom,
Say every word as though I would reply.[83]

Augustus himself, primarily a statesman, did not possess the talent to produce masterpieces like those of Propertius and his colleagues. But the *princeps*, the moving force behind the literary outburst of his age, could not resist the urge to try his hand at writing and turned out a number of works in various literary forms. These included essays such as *Reply to Brutus's Eulogy of Cato* and *An Encouragement to the Study of Philosophy*, a historical work titled *My Autobiography*, and some short poems, *Sicily* and *Epigrams*. Augustus also attempted to write a play but, as Suetonius recorded, this effort came to nothing:

Growing dissatisfied with his tragedy, *Ajax*, which he had begun in great excitement, he destroyed it. When friends asked: "Well, what has Ajax been doing lately?" he answered: "Ajax has fallen on my sponge." [The custom was to use a sponge to erase wet ink from parchment.][84]

Unfortunately, like *Ajax*, all but one of Augustus's writings were lost over the ages. His only surviving work, which may contain a few brief excerpts from his autobiography, was the short, concise, and rather matter-of-fact *Res gestae*, the summary of his main deeds he ordered carved on his tomb.

While Augustus's personal writings disappeared, many of the works of the talented writers who thrived under his and his friends' generous patronage survived to enrich future generations. Ironically, in the long list of accomplishments he listed in the *Res gestae*, including staging gladiator fights, taking a census of the population, and establishing new Roman colonies, there is no mention of his support for writers and intellectuals. Yet the priceless contributions these talented artists made to world literature turned out to be one of his greatest gifts to posterity.

Virgil, Horace, and Varius meet at the home of their distinguished patron, Gaius Maecenas. In addition to epic poems in honor of Julius Caesar and Augustus, Varius wrote the poem On Death, *which expressed philosophical themes, and the theatrical tragedy* Thyestes.

6 Policies and Precedents: Dealing with Dilemmas at Home and Abroad

During his long reign, Augustus faced many political, social, and economic problems, both foreign and domestic, and developed policies to deal with them. In the area of foreign relations, his two most pressing problems were how to govern Rome's many and often distant provinces efficiently and how to establish a strong, safe northern border for the empire. The border problem was particularly significant and became the centerpiece of his foreign policy. In western Europe, the mighty Rhine River was the recognized division between the Roman provinces in Gaul and the rest of northern Europe, a vast expanse of untamed mountains, forests, and plains. These lands were populated by several tribal, seminomadic peoples the Romans referred to collectively as *Germani*, or Germans. Because the Germans had no cities, paved roads, or high culture, the Romans also called them barbarians.

Since the second century B.C., the Germans had posed a potential threat to the empire's northern frontiers, particularly to Gaul, which they raided periodically. Augustus desired to extend these frontiers northward and eastward in order to create a stronger barrier to German aggressions. This passage from the *Res gestae* suggests that he accomplished his goal:

I extended the frontiers of all the provinces of the Roman people. . . . I restored peace to the Gallic and Spanish provinces and likewise to Germany. . . . My fleet sailed the Ocean [the North Sea] from the mouth of the Rhine eastward as far as the territory of the Cimbrians [a German tribe], to which no Roman previously had penetrated either by land or sea. The Cimbrians . . . and other German peoples of the same region . . . sought my friendship and that of the Roman people.[85]

This statement constituted another example of Augustus's skilled use of propaganda, for it glossed over the facts and hid the ugly truth that his efforts in Germany were largely a failure. That failure would have unforeseen and important consequences for the future of the Roman Empire.

Augustus's policy in a key domestic issue also set an important precedent for Rome's future. This issue, one of the most difficult domestic problems he faced, involved the succession of power after his death. Because he had created a new and unique political role—in effect, that of emperor in all but name—no legal rule or precedent existed for the transfer of power. His solution to this dilemma set a pattern that many of his successors would follow, allowing them to perpetuate the imperial political structure he had created.

Administering the Provinces

It is hardly surprising that managing the provinces and policing the borders were the priority issues in Augustus's foreign policy agenda. In the early years of his reign, the empire was a huge, far-flung collection of dozens of diverse lands and peoples. In the far west, bordering the Atlantic Ocean, were Spain and Gaul. Augustus divided Spain into three provinces: Baectia, Lusitania, and Tarraconensis. In Gaul, much of which his great-uncle Caesar had subdued in the 50s B.C. and which was becoming rapidly Romanized, he organized three new provinces: Belgica, Lugdunensis, and Aquitania. Added to the already existing Narbonese, in what is now southern France, Gaul now comprised four provinces.

The rest of the empire was divided as follows. Across its southern tier stretched northern Africa, composed of four provinces. From west to east they were Numidia, Africa (the former Carthaginian homeland), Cyrenaica, and finally Egypt, recently acquired by Augustus himself. North of Egypt, along the eastern border,

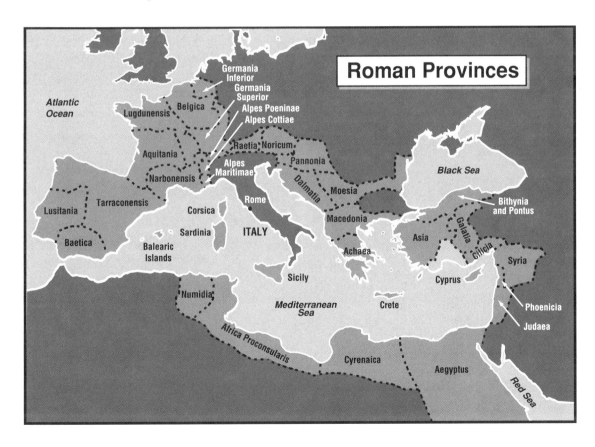

were the provinces of Syria, in northern Palestine, and Asia, Bithynia, Pontus, and Cilicia, all in Asia Minor. West of Asia Minor, across the island-studded Aegean Sea, was Greece, made up of the provinces of Macedonia, Achaea, and Crete. Northwest of Macedonia, along the empire's northern border, was Illyricum (or Dalmatia), then a narrow strip of land bordering the Adriatic Sea, and finally Italy, the Roman heartland.

Outside of that heartland, the vast majority of people were noncitizens who could not take part in consular and other popular elections, exercises that gave Roman citizens at least the illusion of having a say in how they were governed. Most provincials had never even visited Rome or Italy, felt little allegiance to either, and remained under Roman rule mainly because Rome was strong enough to enforce that rule. Thus, organizing and controlling these peoples, not to mention taxing them, was very difficult.

Adding to the task of governing the provinces was the fact that many of them were remote, culturally backward, and had few roads or public services. And they had been poorly administered for a long time. Under the republic, the provincial governors, who were appointed by the Senate and the consuls, served short terms, usually only a year. This did not give them time enough to establish and carry out long-term policies. Moreover, most of these governors, having attained their positions as political favors, were inexperienced, so corruption and mismanagement were common.

Augustus made significant reforms in this system. First, he allowed governors to serve longer so that they could better develop their policies and programs. Also, as historian James Henry Breasted explains:

The governor of a province was now appointed by the permanent ruler at Rome, and . . . knew that he was responsible to that ruler for wise and honest government of his province. He knew also that if he proved successful he could hold his post for years or be promoted to a better one. There thus grew up under the permanent control of Augustus and his successors a body of provincial governors of experience and efficiency.[86]

These abler governors collected more taxes, and less of this revenue ended up in their own pockets, as had often been the case before. The increased flow of money, especially from Egypt and the wealthier provinces, helped the *princeps* to pay his soldiers frequent bonuses and supported his ambitious building programs. Firth lists some of these provincial taxes:

The chief direct taxes were the *tributum soli* and the *tributum capitis*, the former a land tax, paid either in money or in grain, and the latter a personal tax on property or income. . . . In addition to these, there were . . . the 4 percent tax on all inheritances, the 5 percent on . . . every slave, the 1 percent on all commodities sold by auction or in open market, and the 2 percent on the sale of slaves.[87]

Partly to make collecting these taxes more efficient, in the 20s B.C. Augustus ordered a *lustrum*, or census, of the empire's population, the first taken in forty-one years. He recounted this deed with pride in the *Res gestae*: "In my sixth consulship, with Marcus Agrippa as my colleague, I conducted a census of the people. . . . At this *lustrum* 4,063,000 Roman citizens were

This carved relief depicts settlers in a Roman-occupied Germanic province paying taxes in the third century. Many of the provincial policies Augustus introduced were still in effect at this time.

recorded."[88] The figure for the entire population, counting free noncitizens and slaves, has not survived, but was undoubtedly in the tens of millions.

The Parthian and German Frontiers

If Augustus's reform of the provincial system can be called a foreign policy success, it was not his only one. He also succeeded in making peace with a longtime Roman enemy. This was the Parthian Empire, a restored version of the older Persian Empire, centered beyond Palestine in what is now Iran. In the 70s B.C., the Romans and Parthians had begun quarreling over border lands east of Asia Minor and in 53 B.C. a Roman army led by the triumvir Marcus Crassus invaded Parthia. The Parthians delivered him a disastrous defeat, killed him, and captured the battle flags of the

beaten legions. The Romans considered losing these standards a terrible disgrace. In the 30s B.C., in an attempt to gain a glorious reputation, Mark Antony launched another invasion of Parthia, but he met with little more success than Crassus and failed to recover the lost standards.

The Parthian problem remained an open sore, one Augustus had to deal with to retain his credibility and prestige. But he realized that invading Parthia would be expensive and slow down his many domestic programs and reforms. Wisely, he showed restraint; in 20 B.C. he offered Parthian leaders the olive branch of peace. A subsequent treaty provided that existing borders would be honored as long as the Parthians returned the captured flags, which they did, greatly boosting Augustus's prestige at home. Dio Cassius recorded:

> Augustus received the standards . . . as though he had defeated the Parthians in a campaign; he took great pride in

the settlement, and declared that he had won back without striking a blow what had earlier been lost in battle. Indeed, he gave orders that sacrifices should be voted in honor of his success and that a temple for Mars . . . in which the standards were to be dedicated, should be built on the Capitol.[89]

But such successes were ultimately overshadowed by the failure to establish a strong and safe border with the German lands in the north. When Augustus came to power, the northern border was a ragged, ill-defined frontier that ran west-to-east through the central and northern Alps and then dipped southeastward along the upper boundary of Illyricum. Like other Roman leaders, Augustus felt that having the Germans so near the Italian homeland was intolerably dangerous. About 150 miles north of the existing frontier, the powerful Danube River cut horizontally across Europe. This, Augustus reasoned, would constitute a more distant, more easily defended, and therefore safer barrier against the barbarians. Beginning in the mid-20s B.C., Roman armies slowly advanced northward, gaining control of the Alpine valleys, expanding Illyricum's frontier, and establishing new towns in secured areas.

These campaigns increased in size and momentum in 15 B.C. when Augustus's two stepsons, who were both very capable generals, took charge. They were Nero Tiberius Drusus, called Tiberius, and Nero Claudius Drusus, who became known as Drusus the Elder.[90] They eventually extended Roman control to the Danube, fulfilling Augustus's goal. Part of the newly conquered territory went to increase the size of Illyricum and the rest became new

Tiberius (43 B.C.–A.D. 37), Augustus's successor, ruled Rome from A.D. 14 to 37. Thanks to the historians Tacitus and Suetonius, his reign was well documented.

provinces: from west to east, Raetia, Noricum, Pannonia, and Moesia.

From Triumph to Disaster

The northern operations and territorial acquisitions might have made Augustus's German policy an overwhelming success had the Danube frontier remained quiet. But it did not. Almost immediately, German tribes began launching disorganized but destructive raids across the borders, one of them a serious incursion into Gaul. In 12 B.C. Augustus responded by sending Drusus across the Rhine into the heart of German territory, the wild lands sandwiched between that river in the west, the Danube in the south, and the Elbe River in the east. According to Dio:

The enemy harassed him with am-bushes throughout his march, and once even trapped him in a narrow pass . . . indeed, they would have anni-hilated [his army] had not the tribes-men felt seized with contempt for the Romans, regarding them as already captured and only awaiting the finish-ing stroke; this led them to abandon their [battle] formation . . . and brought about their defeat. After this reverse, they no longer showed much confidence, but merely skirmished with the Romans from a distance.[91]

With the Germans more or less intimi-dated, Drusus captured much territory, and three years after crossing the Rhine he camped his army 250 miles away on the Elbe. After this triumph he might have gone on to subdue and Romanize all of Germany; however, a few months later he suddenly and unexpectedly died (ancient sources differ on the cause).

In his brother's stead, Tiberius rushed to the frontier. To send the Germans the message that Drusus's death did not lessen Roman resolve to hold on to the re-gion, he put on a show of force, marching his army back and forth from the Rhine to the Elbe. After that, the area remained rel-atively quiet for a few years, calm enough, in fact, that by A.D. 7 Augustus felt confi-dent about organizing it into a new province. He sent Publius Quintilius Varus, a former consul, to accomplish the task.

The problem was that Varus was an ar-rogant and tactless individual. As Dio re-lated, he quickly abused and angered the German tribes:

When Quintilius Varus became gover-nor of the [planned] province of Ger-

many . . . he tried both to hasten and to widen the process of change. He not only gave orders to the Germans as if they were actual slaves of the Ro-mans, but also levied money from them as if they were subject nations. These were demands they would not tolerate. . . . They did not rise in open rebellion, because they saw that there were many Roman troops near the Rhine and many within their own ter-ritory. Instead, they received [went along with] Varus, and by pretending that they would comply with all his or-ders, they lured him far away from the Rhine.[92]

In A.D. 9, in the dense Teutoburg Forest, located about eighty miles east of the Rhine, a massive German horde, led by a twenty-five-year-old named Arminius, sur-rounded Varus and his troops. The fierce, longhaired German warriors then closed in from all sides and wiped out the Roman force of three legions—at least fifteen thousand soldiers—to the last man.

The news of the disaster struck Rome like a mighty hammer. No Roman army had been so completely defeated in more than two centuries. While grief-stricken crowds gathered in the streets, the usually calm and collected Augustus exploded in an emotional outburst. Dio's account claimed:

At the time when Augustus learned of the disaster which had befallen Varus, he rent [tore at] his clothes, according to some reports, and was overcome with grief. His feelings were not only of sorrow for the soldiers who had per-ished, but of fear for [the safety of] the provinces of Germany and Gaul.[93]

Surrounded on All Sides

In this excerpt from his Roman History, *Dio Cassius described the last hours of the ill-fated Roman army under the command of Publius Varus in Germany's dense Teutoburg Forest.*

"A violent downpour and storm developed, so that the column [of soldiers] was strung out [over a distance]; this also caused the ground around the tree-roots . . . to become slippery, making movement very dangerous. . . . While the Romans were struggling against the elements, the barbarians suddenly surrounded them on all sides at once, stealing through the densest thickets, as they were familiar with the paths. At first they hurled their spears from a distance . . . [and then] closed in to shorter range; for their own part the Roman troops . . . were everywhere overwhelmed by their opponents [and] suffered many casualties and were quite unable to counterattack. . . . They could neither draw their bows nor hurl their javelins to any effect, nor even make use of their shields, which were completely sodden with rain. . . . Besides this the enemy's numbers had been greatly reinforced . . . [making] it easier to encircle and strike down the Romans, whose ranks . . . had lost many men. . . . So every soldier and every horse was cut down."

Suetonius's version supplied other details: "It is said that he took the disaster so deeply to heart that he left his hair and beard untrimmed for months; he would often beat his head on a door, shouting: 'Quintilius Varus, give me back my legions!'"[94]

Varus could not give the legions back, of course, and in fact no one, including Augustus, could replace them. Raising, outfitting, and training three entire legions was simply too costly a proposition, even for someone as wealthy as Augustus. The only way he could have done it would have been to sharply increase taxes, a move he avoided for fear of inciting un-

rest all over the empire. Thus, thanks to Varus's incompetence, for many years to come the Roman army operated with twenty-five instead of twenty-eight legions.

Varus's defeat would have other, even more important consequences for Rome's future. In the following years, the Romans became discouraged, wrote off Germany as a loss, and withdrew their forces from the Elbe back to the Rhine, allowing the natives to regain control of the area. The result was that the Germans never became Romanized. Permanently retaining their independence, they would nurture a deep contempt for Rome and prove a dangerous threat in centuries to come.

The Succession

About the time of the catastrophe in Germany, Augustus had to deal with the most distressing personal problem he had ever faced. He was now in his seventies, physically frail and weak, and he knew that death was a more and more immediate prospect. That meant that a successor was needed to assume the awesome powers and responsibilities of the imperial office he had created. To die without a legal heir might prove disastrous, for the army would then be leaderless and the way would be clear for ambitious generals to vie for control and initiate a new civil war. If his new and better Roman order was to be preserved, Augustus reasoned, he had to have a successor. Because he had no traditional or legal precedent to guide him, he decided to choose someone and then persuade the Senate to accept his nominee.

The burning question was whom to choose. The *princeps* felt that his successor must be either a relative or close friend, for these were the only people he could trust to carry on his programs and to maintain the integrity of the *Principate*. But the men he most loved and trusted had displayed an unfortunate tendency to die on him. His beloved nephew Marcellus (who had married his daughter Julia, making the boy Augustus's son-in-law as well) had died in 23 B.C. Agrippa had been the next logical choice for successor, but he had died in 12 B.C. Before his death, Agrippa too had married Julia, and Augustus became very fond of their sons, Gaius Caesar and Lucius Caesar; however, Lucius died from disease in A.D. 2 and Gaius succumbed to wounds received on a military expedition two years later. Augustus's stepson Drusus, of course, had died in 9 B.C. shortly after leading his army to the Elbe.

That left the other stepson, Tiberius, who was already in his fifties, as the only logical choice to succeed Augustus. Unfortunately, Tiberius was a withdrawn, humorless individual who did not like or interact well with most people. Yet as a general he had proven himself a capable leader and he was also very honest, hardworking, and morally straight, so there was every reason to believe he would govern well. Therefore, over the course of a few years Augustus took several steps designed to bolster his stepson's power and prestige in preparation for the succession. According to the Roman historian Tacitus:

> Nero Drusus [the Elder] was long dead. Tiberius was the only surviving stepson; and everything pointed in his direction [to be Augustus's successor]. He was [legally] adopted as the emperor's son and as partner in his powers (with civil and military authority and the powers of a tribune [awarded for a period of ten years]) and displayed to all the armies.[95]

"Pray Applaud, and Send Me . . . on My Way"

Seemingly satisfied that the problem of the succession had been solved, Augustus carried on his duties as usual. But his health continued to deteriorate and he grew increasingly weak. Eventually, it became too difficult for him to make his accustomed daily visits to the Senate, so he began conducting business from his house on the Palatine. In early August A.D. 14, he felt a bit better and agreed to accompany Tiberius to Beneventum, in south-central Italy, from which the younger man was planning to depart for the province of Illyricum. After bidding his stepson farewell, the *princeps* decided to enjoy a brief holiday and visited nearby Naples before returning to Rome.

At Nola, eighteen miles from Naples, Augustus suddenly became so ill that he could no longer travel. His companions took him to an Octavii family villa that happened to be in Nola and put him to bed in the very room in which his father had died. Augustus must have sensed that his own death was near, for he sent a messenger to recall Tiberius as quickly as possible. Rushing to the scene, Tiberius conversed at length with his stepfather; though their words were never recorded, it is probable that the older man gave the younger some last-minute advice about governing the empire.

A few hours later, the *princeps* summoned friends and family members present to come close to his bedside. "Have I played my part in the farce of life creditably enough?"[96] he asked weakly. When they tearfully answered that he had, he added the well-known tag line often used to end Roman comedies in the theater: "Since well I've played my part, then, gentle people, pray applaud, and send me with your thanks on my way."[97] Finally, he embraced Livia and, in a barely audible whisper, asked her never to forget their deep love and long marriage. Seconds later, he died in her arms. According to Suetonius, "Augustus died in the same room as his father Octavius. That was 19

Livia attends her husband at his deathbed. Dignified and personable, she was devoted to both Augustus and her son, Tiberius, and gained increased political influence after the latter succeeded Augustus as emperor. When she died, the Senate ordered an arch erected to honor her memory.

August, A.D. 14, at about 3 p.m. . . . In thirty-five days' time he would have attained the age of seventy-six."[98]

Saddened by Augustus's passing, the Roman nation grieved more solemnly and more openly than it had for any past leader. On the journey back to Rome, local officials from each town along the way took charge of the body in their turn, bearing it proudly while tens of thousands of silent mourners lined the roadway. After a short ceremony at the Julii family shrine, located twelve miles outside the capital, the mourners entered the city and placed Augustus's body in his house.

The next day Tiberius, dressed in black, summoned a session of the Senate, and the Roman fathers discussed the honors they would bestow upon Augustus. They decreed that henceforth his reign should be known as the "Augustan Age" and so noted on the Roman calendar. He would also be deified, or officially declared a god, temples would be dedicated to him, statues of him erected, and the house in Nola where he had died made holy ground. At the close of the meeting, Tiberius's son Drusus, also dressed in black, solemnly read the entire *Res gestae* aloud to the senators.

A Lone Eagle Ascending

Then the formal funeral procession began. Dio recorded:

A couch was made of ivory and gold and spread with a pall [cloth] of purple and gold. Beneath the covering his body was hidden in a coffin; above it a wax effigy, clad in triumphal dress, was displayed. . . . Behind these were conveyed the images of Augustus's ancestors, of his deceased relatives . . . and finally those of the other Romans of the past who had distinguished themselves in some way, beginning with Romulus himself.[99]

The massive, solemn, and silent procession, made up of all the senators, the entire Praetorian Guard, and many thousands of citizens, descended the Palatine Hill and wound its way through the crowd-lined streets to the main Forum. It then moved past the temples of Vesta and Janus to the temple built to honor Julius Caesar's memory. There the mourners halted to allow Tiberius to deliver an emotional and respectful funeral oration.

Then the procession, now swollen in number to well over a hundred thousand mourners, continued. It passed under the Capitoline Hill, on which rested the magnificent temples Augustus had built for Jupiter, through a triumphal arch, and into the Campus Martius. There, the mourners placed the coffin on a huge wooden pyre. After tossing onto the pyre the medals they had won in combat, a gesture of respect and final farewell, a group of veteran soldiers used torches to set the pyre ablaze. As the flames began to engulf the coffin, a lone eagle was released into the sky, a symbol of Augustus's spirit ascending into heaven. And at the same moment, while many onlookers wept openly, a choir of children, hundreds strong, began singing a beautiful hymn for the dead. "When these ceremonies had been completed," wrote Dio, "all the others departed, but Livia remained on the spot for five days. . . . Then she had his bones gathered up and placed in his tomb."[100]

Glory for All Time

During Augustus's magnificent funeral procession, his successor, Tiberius, delivered a moving oration, paying tribute to the many good deeds of Rome's most beloved leader. The exact words of the speech are unknown, but Dio Cassius included a paraphrase, from which this excerpt is taken, in his Roman History.

"He [Augustus] could by virtue of . . . the armed strength and the money at his command have proclaimed himself the supreme and sole ruler. . . . Yet he refused, and . . . first brought back to health and then returned to your keeping the whole system of [republican] government. . . . He provided for [the Roman people] public works, distributions of money, games, festivals . . . an abundance of the necessities of life, and security, not only from wrongdoers and foreign enemies, but even from the acts of the gods. . . . How too could I forget to mention a man who lived his private life in poverty and used his wealth only for public service; who treated himself with austerity but others with lavish generosity; who took upon his own shoulders every hardship and danger for your sake . . . who on holidays received even the masses into his own house. . . . How could I pass over the multitude of laws which he enacted. . . . They offered to those who had suffered wrong compensations that were sufficient, and for the wrongdoers penalties that were not inhuman. . . . This, then, was why you had good reason to make him your leader and the father of the people, why you honored him with so many distinctions . . . and why you finally made him a demi-god and declared him to be immortal. And so it is right that we should not mourn for him, but that while we now return his body to nature, we should glorify his spirit for all time as that of a divine being."

Tiberius as a young military general, wearing a laurel wreath to commemorate a victory.

A reconstruction of Augustus's tomb, which stood in the Campus Martius in Rome. The structure was composed largely of Roman concrete and topped with a bronze statue of the deceased emperor.

The Roman people gave Augustus so many heartfelt honors in death because he had given them so much in life. In his youth he had risen ruthlessly through the corridors of power to become an all-powerful dictator. But once in power, unlike most other absolute rulers, he had ruled fairly, wisely, and constructively. Tacitus concisely summed up the tone and breadth of his achievements in these lines:

> Augustus had put the State in order not by making himself king . . . but by creating the *Principate*. [Under his rule] the empire's frontiers were on the ocean, or distant rivers. Armies, provinces, fleets, the whole system was interrelated [well organized and administered]. Roman citizens were protected by the law. Provincials were decently treated. Rome itself had been lavishly beautified. Force had been sparingly used—merely to preserve peace for the majority.[101]

Considering this admirable and impressive record, Augustus need not have worried about his role in the farce of life. Indeed, he had played his part exceedingly well.

Rome's Spirit Lives On

The Roman Empire, which Augustus had almost single-handedly created, bore the indelible imprint of his ideas and works for centuries. On the political front, the *Principate* not only endured, but slowly grew in scope and power until Rome's leaders were nothing less than absolute dictators who openly and unashamedly used the title of emperor. Yet most Romans were satisfied with this arrangement. For one thing, because Augustus had ruled so efficiently and benevolently, nearly all desires and ambitions to bring back true republican government had died out during his reign.

Also, for a majority of people life was secure and reasonably happy. For nearly two centuries after Augustus's death, the empire was prosperous and living standards, especially for the upper classes, were higher than in republican times. Even the poor benefited, thanks to the program of bread and circuses the emperors maintained and often expanded. And the whole Mediterranean world remained relatively peaceful, so that the era spanning the first two imperial centuries came to be called the *Pax Romana,* or Great Roman Peace, a larger extension of the *Pax Augustae.*

The second century A.D. was especially prosperous, peaceful, and secure, thanks

to five unusually able emperors: Nerva, Trajan, Hadrian, Antoninus Pius, and Marcus Aurelius. They each ruled with the same kind of integrity, efficiency, and generosity Augustus had. In his monumental *Decline and Fall of the Roman Empire,* the great historian Edward Gibbon wrote:

> If a man were called to fix [choose] the period in the history of the world during which the condition of the human race was most happy and prosperous, he would, without hesitation, name that which elapsed from the accession of Nerva [in 98] to the death of Aurelius [in 180]. Their united reigns are possibly the only period of history in which the happiness of a great people was the sole object of government.[102]

This may seem an overstatement considering that during these years slavery remained widespread and the early Christians were periodically persecuted. But the fact is that since that century the Mediterranean/European world has by far never witnessed so long an era in which there were no national borders, no separate governments, no trade tariffs, and no wars. It is hardly surprising, then, that almost no one who lived under the sheltering wing of the Roman eagle during the *Pax Ro-*

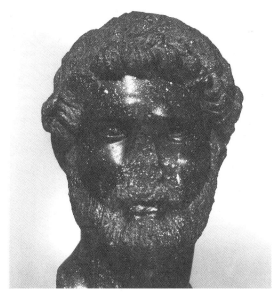

The emperors Trajan (left) and Hadrian were unusually fair, enlightened, and constructive rulers.

mana opposed the continuing autocratic rule of the emperors.

Crisis, Turmoil, and Decay

Eventually, however, even the immense wealth, prestige, and military powers of these rulers could not cope with the mounting problems the empire began to face near the close of the second century. During the three centuries that followed, the Roman world experienced almost unending crisis, turmoil, and steady decay. This was partly the result of increasingly poor leadership. In contrast to the honest and able rulers of the second century, most of the later emperors were brutal, ambitious, and/or incompetent men who had little or no concept of governing so large a realm.

Another problem was a steady breakdown of military discipline. The once strong and efficient Roman military grew increasingly more disorganized, ineffective, and sometimes even disloyal. Often, army factions or the Praetorian Guard, once Augustus's trustworthy right arm, ran amok, choosing new emperors or disposing of old ones at will.

The economy declined, too, and on several occasions reached the brink of collapse. Political instability, as well as new wars and piracy, both of which the weakened army could not prevent, disrupted trade. And at the same time farming declined, causing food shortages and price increases, while the inefficient government wasted money and tried to make up its losses by overtaxing the populace.

The net result of these crises was a periodic breakdown in law and order, a sharp increase in poverty, and widespread insecurity and uncertainty. The empire reached a low ebb of chaos and misery in the mid–third century. As James Breasted describes it:

For fifty years there was no public order, as the plundering troops tossed the scepter [symbol of ruling power] of Rome from one soldier-emperor to another. Life and property were nowhere safe; turbulence, robbery, and murder were everywhere. The tumult and fighting between rival emperors hastened the ruin of all business; and as the affairs of the nation passed from bad to worse, national bankruptcy ensued.[103]

In the late third and early fourth centuries, a handful of stronger leaders, most notably the emperor Diocletian, managed to restore a temporary semblance of order. But their attempts to halt and reverse the empire's destructive downward spiral proved too little too late. The barbarians were already at the gate.

Rome's Demise

In the fourth and fifth centuries, the failure of Augustus and his successors to subdue and Romanize Germany came back to haunt the empire. Since Augustus's time, the northern tribes had grown more populous, more organized, and much more restless. "By the fourth century," Chester Starr writes,

there stretched along the Roman frontier from west to east the Franks (lower Rhine), Alamanni (southern

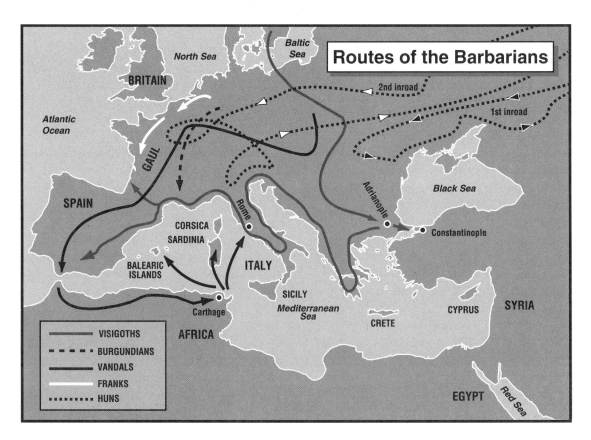

Germany), Vandals (Hungary), and the Goths reaching on into Russia. . . . Behind these, in dim darkness from the Roman point of view, were the Burgundians, the Saxons, the Lombards, and other tribes.[104]

One after another, these peoples poured in waves over the empire's northern borders.

An ordered, militarily strong, and highly patriotic and resilient society like that of Augustan Rome might have stopped these waves. But it was a sick, disorganized, and weakened empire, a mere shell of its former self, that faced the onslaught of the fifth century's huge barbarian invasions. In 408 the Goths sacked Rome; the Vandals did the same in 455. After this, many city-dwellers fled into the countryside, the city's administrative and public services, already nearly nonexistent, broke down completely, and Rome's population quickly shrank from more than a million to less than twenty thousand. In 476, yet another wave of invaders forced the last Roman emperor, a fearful and powerless fourteen-year-old boy named Romulus Augustus, to vacate the throne.

There was great irony in that name. The legendary Romulus had founded the city-state that had grown into the stately Roman Republic and Augustus, greatest of all Roman leaders, had created the Roman Empire. Now this unfortunate youth bearing their names presided over the final pathetic demise of Roman power. Because of his youth, many called him Augustulus, or "Little Augustus."

The other ironic link between Augustus and Augustulus was that each faced and failed to stop the German threat. This

The Vandals attack and pillage Rome in A.D. *455, an act for which their name became synonymous with senseless destruction.*

failure was perfectly understandable in the case of the last emperor. But the first Augustus possessed the power and resources to absorb northern Europe into the Roman sphere. And though he had no way to predict the eventual consequences, his failure to follow through with this policy after the massacre of Varus's army proved to be one of history's most serious miscalculations. In view of the final triumph of the northern tribes over Rome, then, the encounter in the Teutoberg Forest in A.D. 9 ranks as one of the most crucial and decisive battles in world history.

A Grand Dream Fulfilled

Yet this single major failure of Augustus was, in a sense, outweighed by his many successes. Under his rule, Roman architecture, law, and literature reached high levels of excellence and the glory and nobility of Roman civilization was fixed forever in the human imagination. Though Rome fell to the barbarians, much of Roman culture, including the works and ideals of the Augustan Age, survived. The European kingdoms that grew from the empire's wreckage retained many Roman customs, institutions, and ideas, as well as the Latin language, which eventually mutated into French and other modern tongues. Europe also kept alive the memory of the mighty world order Augustus had built and the prosperous and happy *Pax Romana* he had initiated.

The overriding theme of that order and that age was the grand destiny of Rome, which was seen as an eternal thought in the minds of the gods. Ovid expressed this confident and patriotic idea when he wrote:

Even as I speak I see our destiny,
The city of our sons and sons of sons,
Greater than any city we have known,

A Living Army Buries a Dead One

The deaths of the Roman soldiers in the battle in the Teutoburg Forest was particularly upsetting for their relatives because the bodies were never recovered. The mourners felt some measure of closure when, in A.D. 15, Germanicus, son of Drusus the Elder, led an expedition to the site of the disaster and buried the victims' remains. Tacitus described it in this excerpt from his Annals.

"Now they were near the Teutoburg Wood, in which the remains of Varus and his three divisions were said to be lying unburied. Germanicus [desired] to pay his last respects to these men and their general. Every soldier with him was overcome with pity when he thought of his relations and friends and reflected on the hazards of war and of human life. . . . Then the army made its way over the tragic site. The scene lived up to its horrible reputation. . . . On the open ground were whitening bones, scattered where men had fled, heaped up where they had stood and fought back. Fragments of spears and of horses' limbs lay there—also human heads, fastened to tree trunks. In groves nearby were the outlandish altars at which the Germans had massacred the Roman officers. . . . So, six years after the slaughter, a living Roman army had come to bury the dead men's bones of three whole divisions. No one knew if the remains he was burying belonged to a stranger or a comrade. But in their bitter distress, and rising fury against the enemy, they looked on them all as friends and blood-brothers."

Like a moment frozen forever in time, this vivid vignette from a Roman celebration captures the splendor of Augustan Rome and the vitality and supreme confidence of a great people at their cultural zenith.

Or has been known or shall be known to men.[105]

Augustus and other eloquent Roman spokesmen—Virgil, Livy, and their literary colleagues—promoted this magnificent vision of the Roman spirit living on eternally. And indeed, through Rome's profound cultural legacy to Europe, that spirit still dwells comfortably within the fabric of Western civilization. In a way Rome never fell, but merely passed from the world of flesh and blood into the realm of thought and ideas. And in this way, one even the brilliant Augustus could not have foreseen, his grand dream of an immortal Rome was fulfilled.

Notes

Introduction: A Complex and Remarkable Individual

1.   J. Wight Duff, *A Literary History of Rome from the Origins to the Close of the Golden Age.* New York: Barnes and Noble, 1963, p. 352.

2.   Chester G. Starr, *The Ancient Romans.* New York: Oxford University Press, 1971, p. 104.

3.   Quoted in Donald R. Dudley, *The Romans: 850 B.C.–A.D. 337.* New York: Knopf, 1970, p. 147.

4.   Quoted in William G. Sinnegen, ed., *Sources in Western Civilization: Rome.* New York: The Free Press, 1965, p. 109.

5.   Henry Thompson Rowell, *Rome in the Augustan Age.* Norman: University of Oklahoma Press, 1962, p. 9.

Chapter 1: The Jungle of Roman Politics: Octavian's Rise to Ultimate Power

6.   Rowell, *Rome in the Augustan Age*, pp. 14–15.

7.   Suetonius, *Lives of the Twelve Caesars*, published as *The Twelve Caesars.* Translated by Robert Graves and revised by Michael Grant. New York: Penguin Books, 1979, pp. 98–99.

8.   Virgil, *Aeneid.* Translated by Patric Dickinson. New York: New American Library, 1961, p. 7.

9.   The Romans reckoned their dates using the letters A.U.C., which stood for *ab urbe condita,* or "from the founding of the city." Following this system, Romulus founded Rome in 1 A.U.C. and the birth of Christ, now dated as A.D. 1, took place in 754 A.U.C.

10.   Virgil, *Aeneid*, pp. 13–14.

11.   Starr, *The Ancient Romans*, p. 57.

12.   Starr, *The Ancient Romans*, p. 15.

13.   John Buchan, *Augustus.* London: Hodder and Stoughton, 1937, pp. 27–29.

14.   Buchan, *Augustus*, p. 29.

15.   Appian, *Roman History.* Translated by Horace White. Cambridge, MA: Harvard University Press, 1964, p. 176.

16.   Donald Earl, *The Age of Augustus.* New York: Crown Publishers, 1968, p. 29.

17.   John B. Firth, *Augustus Caesar and the Organization of the Empire of Rome.* Freeport, NY: Books for the Libraries Press, 1972, pp. 75–77.

18.   Quoted in Sinnegen, *Sources in Western Civilization*, p. 105.

19.   Dudley, *The Romans*, p. 141.

20.   Buchan, *Augustus*, p. 122.

Chapter 2: Rescuing an Upside-Down Age: The Bold New Augustan Order

21.   Quoted in Dudley, *The Romans*, p. 139.

22.   Dio Cassius, *Roman History.* Translated by Ian Scott-Kilvert. New York: Penguin, 1987, p. 79.

23.   Quoted in Dio Cassius, *Roman History*, p. 100.

24.   Buchan, *Augustus*, p. 33.

25.   Quoted in Dio Cassius, *Roman History*, p. 123.

26.   Firth, *Augustus Caesar*, p. 165.

27.   Dio Cassius, *Roman History*, p. 128.

28.   Dio Cassius, *Roman History*, p. 140.

29.   This was not without precedent. In the 40s B.C., the Senate had changed the preceding month, *Quintilis*, to Julius (now July), to honor the dictator Julius Caesar.

30.   Quoted in Suetonius, *The Twelve Caesars*, p. 69.

31.   Rowell, *Rome in the Augustan Age*, pp. 64–65.

32.   Buchan, *Augustus*, p. 137.

33. Michael Grant, *The Army of the Caesars.* New York: M. Evans and Company, 1974, p. 56.

34. Dudley, *The Romans*, p. 144.

35. Dio Cassius, *Roman History*, p. 144.

36. Dio Cassius, *Roman History*, p. 145.

37. Quoted in Suetonius, *The Twelve Caesars*, p. 87.

38. Firth, *Augustus Caesar*, p. 180.

Chapter 3: From Town of Bricks to City of Marble: Transforming the Roman Capital

39. Suetonius, *The Twelve Caesars*, p. 69.

40. Quoted in Rowell, *Rome in the Augustan Age*, p. 120.

41. Quoted in Jerome Carcopino, *Daily Life in Ancient Rome: The People and the City at the Height of the Empire.* New Haven, CT: Yale University Press, 1940, p. 25.

42. Earl, *The Age of Augustus*, p. 88.

43. Dio Cassius, *Roman History*, p. 145.

44. Rome's first sewer, the *cloaca maxima*, was constructed about the year 575 B.C. under the supervision of the Etruscans, who ruled the city at the time. The sixteen-foot-wide semicircular arch at its spillway into the Tiber still exists in nearly perfect condition.

45. Rowell, *Rome in the Augustan Age*, pp. 126–27.

46. Earl, *The Age of Augustus*, p. 99.

47. Quoted in Sinnegen, *Sources in Western Civilization*, p. 109.

48. Suetonius, *The Twelve Caesars*, p. 70.

49. Suetonius, *The Twelve Caesars*, pp. 71–72.

50. Dudley, *The Romans*, p. 146.

51. Quoted in Earl, *The Age of Augustus*, p. 102.

52. Quoted in Sinnegen, *Sources in Western Civilization*, p. 107.

53. Rowell, *Rome in the Augustan Age*, p. 161.

54. Quoted in Sinnegen, *Sources in Western Civilization*, p. 110.

55. Quoted in R. H. Barrow, *The Romans.* Baltimore: Penguin, 1949, p. 85.

Chapter 4: Restoring Roman Family Values: Augustus's Moral Crusade

56. Earl, *The Age of Augustus*, p. 166.

57. Suetonius, *The Twelve Caesars*, p. 103.

58. Rowell, *Rome in the Augustan Age*, p. 197.

59. Firth, *Augustus Caesar*, p. 207.

60. Yet, like Greek women, Roman women could not vote or hold public office, rights exclusive to free adult men. On the other hand, free women in Rome *could* appear as witnesses in court cases, a privilege denied Greek women.

61. Rowell, *Rome in the Augustan Age*, pp. 202–205.

62. Firth, *Augustus Caesar*, pp. 217–18.

63. Suetonius, *The Twelve Caesars*, p. 81.

64. Suetonius, *The Twelve Caesars*, p. 97.

65. Suetonius, *The Twelve Caesars*, p. 84.

66. Earl, *The Age of Augustus*, p. 168.

67. Earl, *The Age of Augustus*, p. 175.

Chapter 5: Triumph of the Spirit: The Golden Age of Roman Literature

68. Suetonius, *The Twelve Caesars*, p. 103.

69. Garry Wills, ed., *Roman Culture: Weapons and the Man.* New York: George Braziller, 1966, p. 25.

70. Michael Grant, *The World of Rome.* New York: New American Library, 1960, p. 234.

71. Their direct precursor was the late republican poet Gaius Catullus (ca. 84–ca. 54 B.C.), who pined for his mistress Lesbia after she had dumped him for another man. The only surviving copy of his works was discovered in the late 1200s stuffed in an old wine barrel.

72. Firth, *Augustus Caesar*, pp. 208–209.

73. Virgil, *Aeneid*, pp. 142–43.

74. Barrow, *The Romans*, pp. 85–86.

75. Dudley, *The Romans*, p. 178.

76. Quoted in Wills, *Roman Culture*, p. 295.

77. Bernard Knox, ed., *The Norton Book of Classical Literature*. New York: W. W. Norton, 1993, p. 53.

78. Quoted in Wills, *Roman Culture*, p. 154.

79. Duff, *A Literary History of Rome*, p. 464.

80. Kevin Guinagh and Alfred Paul Dorjahn, eds., *Latin Literature in Translation*. New York: Longman's, Green, 1952, p. 501.

81. Quoted in Dudley, *The Romans*, p. 178.

82. Livy, *From the Founding of the City*. 14 vols. Translated by Evan T. Sage. Cambridge, MA: Harvard University Press, 1965, pp. 409–11.

83. Quoted in Wills, *Roman Culture*, p. 133.

84. Suetonius, *The Twelve Caesars*, p. 100.

Chapter 6: Policies and Precedents: Dealing with Dilemmas at Home and Abroad

85. Quoted in Sinnegen, *Sources in Western Civilization*, pp. 110–11.

86. James Henry Breasted, *Ancient Times: A History of the Early World*. Boston: Ginn, 1944, p. 683.

87. Firth, *Augustus Caesar*, pp. 226–27.

88. Quoted in Sinnegen, *Sources in Western Civilization*, p. 106.

89. Dio Cassius, *Roman History*, p. 162.

90. Augustus had no sons of his own. Tiberius and Drusus were Livia's sons by a previous marriage.

91. Dio Cassius, *Roman History*, pp. 184–85.

92. Dio Cassius, *Roman History*, pp. 235–36.

93. Dio Cassius, *Roman History*, p. 239.

94. Suetonius, *The Twelve Caesars*, p. 65.

95. Tacitus, *The Annals*, published as *The Annals of Imperial Rome*. Translated by Michael Grant. New York: Penguin, 1989, p. 33.

96. Quoted in Suetonius, *The Twelve Caesars*, p. 110.

97. Quoted in Buchan, *Augustus*, p. 323.

98. Suetonius, *The Twelve Caesars*, p. 110.

99. Dio Cassius, *Roman History*, p. 247.

100. Dio Cassius, *Roman History*, p. 255.

101. Tacitus, *The Annals of Imperial Rome*, pp. 37–38.

Epilogue: Rome's Spirit Lives On

102. Edward Gibbon, *The Decline and Fall of the Roman Empire*, in *Great Books of the Western World*. Vol. 1. Edited by Mortimer J. Adler. Chicago: Encyclopaedia Britannica, 1952, p. 32.

103. Breasted, *Ancient Times*, p. 751.

104. Starr, *The Ancient Romans*, p. 207.

105. Quoted in Wills, *Roman Culture*, p. 245.

For Further Reading

Isaac Asimov, *The Roman Empire*. Boston: Houghton Mifflin, 1967. An excellent, easy-to-read, although brief and general, overview of all aspects of the empire, including the Augustan Age.

Lionel Casson, *Daily Life in Ancient Rome*. New York: American Heritage, 1975. A fascinating presentation of how the Romans lived: their homes, streets, entertainments, eating habits, marriage customs, and more.

Ron Goor and Nancy Goor, *Pompeii: Exploring a Roman Ghost Town*. New York: Thomas Y. Crowell, 1986. An overview of the excavations at Pompeii, a small Roman city that flourished in the Augustan Age and was buried by a volcanic eruption a few decades after Augustus's death. For basic readers.

Anthony Marks and Graham Tingay, *The Romans*. London: Usborne, 1990. Aimed at young readers, this is a very accurate and entertaining summary of Roman history and life, with hundreds of fine color illustrations.

Don Nardo, *The Battle of Actium*. San Diego: Lucent Books, 1996. In what can be considered a companion volume to this book on the Augustan Age, the author traces in more detail Octavian's rise to power, his propaganda war with Antony and Cleopatra, and the bloody showdown between the three at Actium, the battle that gave Octavian control of the whole Roman world and paved the way for the establishment of the *Principate* and the empire.

———, *The Roman Republic*, *The Roman Empire*, and *The Importance of Cleopatra*. San Diego: Lucent Books, 1994; *Greek and Roman Theater*. San Diego: Lucent Books, 1995; and *Life in Ancient Rome*. San Diego: Lucent Books, 1996. These comprehensive but easy-to-read overviews of various aspects of Roman civilization provide a broader context for understanding the Augustan Age, its leaders, and its cultural contributions.

Major Works Consulted

Appian, *Roman History*. Translated by Horace White. Cambridge, MA: Harvard University Press, 1964. After two thousand years, Appian's epic history of Rome's civil wars remains important and riveting reading. Contains much about Caesar, Antony, Octavian, Cleopatra, and other leading figures of the era.

John Buchan, *Augustus*. London: Hodder and Stughton, 1937. Though a bit dated, this book by the late and highly respected Buchan (Lord Tweedsmuir) remains one of the most detailed and thoughtful modern studies of the Augustan Age. The review of the volume in the *London Daily Mail* was right on target in calling it "a masterly and engrossing study . . . told with a flowing sweep and in brilliant language."

Gilbert Charles-Picard, *Augustus and Nero*. Translated from the French by Len Ortzen. New York: Thomas Y. Crowell, 1965. A capable scholar offers some telling insights about the characters and personal lives of two of the most famous Roman emperors.

F. R. Cowell, *Cicero and the Roman Republic*. Baltimore: Penguin, 1967. A very detailed and interesting analysis of the late republic, its leaders, including Octavian, and the problems that eventually led to its collapse.

Dio Cassius, *Roman History*. Translated by Ian Scott-Kilvert. New York: Penguin, 1987. An excellent modern translation of Dio's important work about the events of Augustus Caesar's rise to power and reign as the first Roman emperor. This is one of the key primary sources for the Augustan Age.

Donald R. Dudley, *The Romans: 850 B.C.–A.D. 337*. New York: Knopf, 1970. A very thoughtful overview of Roman history and culture.

Donald Earl, *The Age of Augustus*. New York: Crown Publishers, 1968. A handsome book with numerous photos, some in color. The text is detailed and useful but written in a very scholarly style, making it difficult reading for all but serious Augustus buffs.

John B. Firth, *Augustus Caesar and the Organization of the Empire of Rome*. Freeport, NY: Books for the Libraries Press, 1972. Beginning with Julius Caesar's assassination in 44 B.C., this is a detailed, thoughtful telling of Octavian's rise to power in the civil wars and his ascendancy as Augustus, the first Roman emperor.

Michael Grant, *The Army of the Caesars*. New York: M. Evans and Company, 1974. Grant's detailed study of the evolution of Roman armies, including two fulsome chapters on Augustus's military reforms, is first-rate scholarship.

Henry Thompson Rowell, *Rome in the Augustan Age*. Norman: University of Oklahoma Press, 1962. A well-written synopsis of the history and culture of one of Rome's greatest periods, with a heavy emphasis on religious, social, and moral values.

William G. Sinnegen, ed., *Sources in Western Civilization: Rome*. New York: The

Free Press, 1965. A fine collection of Roman writings, including excerpts from works by Livy, Polybius, Appian, Cicero, Suetonius, and others. Also contains the *Res gestae*, the short but important work written by Augustus himself.

Chester G. Starr, *The Ancient Romans.* New York: Oxford University Press, 1971. A well-written short summary of both the Roman Republic and the Roman Empire. Includes several interesting primary source quotations and a special sidebar on the Augustan Age.

Suetonius, *Lives of the Twelve Caesars*, published as *The Twelve Caesars*. Translated by Robert Graves and revised by Michael Grant. New York: Penguin Books, 1979. Suetonius's biography of Augustus is one of the most important ancient documents about the leader and his deeds.

Garry Wills, ed., *Roman Culture: Weapons and the Man.* New York: George Braziller, 1966. This excellent collection of Latin literature contains works by Virgil, Horace, Ovid, Propertius, and other important Roman writers of the Augustan Age. Also, Wills's long introduction contains much insightful commentary.

Additional Works Consulted

E. Badian, *Roman Imperialism in the Late Republic*. Ithaca, NY: Cornell University Press, 1968.

R. H. Barrow, *The Romans*. Baltimore: Penguin, 1949.

James Henry Breasted, *Ancient Times: A History of the Early World*. Boston: Ginn, 1944.

James H. Butler, *The Theater and Drama of Greece and Rome*. San Francisco: Chandler, 1972.

Jerome Carcopino, *Daily Life in Ancient Rome: The People and the City at the Height of the Empire*. New Haven, CT: Yale University Press, 1940.

Cicero, *Letters to Atticus*. Translated by E. O. Winstedt. Cambridge, MA: Harvard University Press, 1961.

Robert B. Downs, *Books That Changed the World*. New York: Penguin, 1983.

Donald R. Dudley, *The Civilization of Rome*. New York: New American Library, 1960.

J. Wight Duff, *A Literary History of Rome from the Origins to the Close of the Golden Age*. New York: Barnes and Noble, 1963.

Edward Gibbon, *The Decline and Fall of the Roman Empire*, in *Great Books of the Western World*. Vol. 1. Edited by Mortimer J. Adler. Chicago: Encyclopaedia Britannica, 1952.

Michael Grant, *The Founders of the Western World: A History of Greece and Rome*. New York: Scribner's, 1991.

———, *History of Rome*. New York: Scribner's, 1978.

———, *The World of Rome*. New York: New American Library, 1960.

Kevin Guinagh and Alfred Paul Dorjahn, eds., *Latin Literature in Translation*. New York: Longman's, Green, 1952.

Edith Hamilton, *The Roman Way to Western Civilization*. New York: W. W. Norton, 1932.

Bernard Knox, ed., *The Norton Book of Classical Literature*. New York: W. W. Norton, 1993.

Plutarch, *Lives of the Noble Grecians and Romans*. Translated by John Dryden. New York: Random House, 1932.

———, *Lives of the Noble Grecians and Romans*, excerpted in *Plutarch: Fall of the Roman Republic*. Translated by Rex Warner. Baltimore: Penguin, 1958.

Betty Radice, *Who's Who in the Ancient World*. New York: Penguin, 1973.

Meyer Reinhold, *Essentials of Greek and Roman Classics*. Great Neck, NY: Barron's Educational Series, 1946.

Shakespeare, *Julius Caesar*. New York: Washington Square Press, 1959.

Tacitus, *The Annals*, published as *The Annals of Imperial Rome*. Translated by Michael Grant. New York: Penguin, 1989.

Lily Ross Taylor, *Party Politics in the Age of Caesar*. Berkeley: University of California Press, 1968.

Index

Picture Credits

Cover photo: Stock Montage

Archivi Alinari/Art Resource, NY, 49

The Bettmann Archive, 10, 12, 15, 23, 26, 28, 32, 46, 47 (both), 57, 59, 67, 74

The British Museum, 36 (both), 51, 91 (both)

Corbis-Bettmann, 31, 81, 88, 95

Culver Pictures, 27 (left)

Hulton Deutsch, 38

North Wind Picture Archives, 19, 22 (bottom), 27 (right), 39 (bottom), 50, 60, 62, 63, 69, 77

Ny Carlsberg Glyptotek, Copenhagen, 22 (top), 82

Stock Montage, Inc., 14, 18, 21, 43, 52, 54, 58, 71, 73, 74, 86, 89, 93

About the Author

Don Nardo is an award-winning author whose more than seventy books cover a wide range of topics, including science, health, and the environment. His main field, however, is history. Among his modern historical studies are *Braving the New World*, *The Mexican-American War*, *The U.S. Presidency*, and biographies of Thomas Jefferson, Franklin D. Roosevelt, and William Lloyd Garrison. Mr. Nardo's specialty is the ancient world, especially classical Greece and Rome, about which, in addition to this volume on the Augustan Age, he has written *The Battle of Marathon*, *The Age of Pericles*, *Life in Ancient Greece*, *Life in Ancient Rome*, *The Battle of Zama*, *The Punic Wars*, and many others. Mr. Nardo also dabbles periodically in orchestral composition, oil painting, screenwriting, and film directing. He lives with his wife, Christine, on Cape Cod, Massachusetts.